Alison Lane is the youngest of three daughters of a family doctor in Harrow, Middlesex. Now retired, she had a lifelong career in research and development for an international pharma company based in the UK, which she thoroughly enjoyed. Her work was very important to her. She and Simon have two children – the elder, Alex, has Down's syndrome; his loving nature was the inspiration for this book. Charlotte is the younger child, whose birth seemed a miraculous gift.

Alison enjoys a full and active social life in the company of friends and family. She enjoys swimming, entertaining and travel.

DOWN BUT NOT OUT

The First 25 Years

Alison J Lane

DOWN BUT NOT OUT

The First 25 Years

Olympia Publishers
London

www.olympiapublishers.com
OLYMPIA PAPERBACK EDITION

The author has tried to recreate events, circumstances and conversations from her
memories of them. In order to maintain their anonymity, in some instances the
names of individuals, places, identifying characteristics and other details may have
been changed. Every endeavour has been made to seek permission from people,
associations and material mentioned and used, respectively.

A CIP catalogue record for this title is
available from the British Library.

ISBN: 978-1-84897-588-0

(Olympia Publishers is part of Ashwell Publishing Ltd)

First Published in 2015

Olympia Publishers
60 Cannon Street
London
EC4N 6NP

Printed in Great Britain

Acknowledgements

With grateful thanks to my wonderful husband, Simon, for being there, even when he wasn't! (Working, racing/cars/garage tasks.)

To my family, especially my marvellous Mum and late Dad, and our dear friends, Janet and Lietta, for proof-reading this book.

To my sisters, Wendy and Diane, and sisters-in-law, Susan and Katy, who had their own families to care for, yet were unfailingly supportive.

To all our friends, carers and nannies, who helped in so many ways.

I dedicate this book to Alex, my inspiration for this book, Simon, my constant companion and Charlotte, our caring, vibrant daughter, altogether my loving family.

Foreword

Simon and Alison Lane have a twenty-six year old son, Alex, with Down's syndrome, and a daughter, Charlotte, aged twenty-four. They live in Middlesex. Alison's late father, who played a crucial role in their lives, was a GP. This is an account of how Alex came into their lives and changed their future.

Preface

Our gorgeous son, Alex, now twenty-six years old, was born with Down's syndrome. *

Much as we adore him, we wish he did not have that wretched extra chromosome 21, with all the associated characteristics. In truth, it is heart breaking. Alex is extremely happy and seemingly unaware that he is different, but you or I would hate to have that extra chromosome, and so would he if he fully understood the condition.

Most of the time we are a typical family, getting on with jobs and life, and not dwelling on the 'Down's', but it is always there, of course. There are many positives, so please do not despair. Read on and enjoy our story, for Alex is a pleasure and a delight, and his very presence is so uplifting.

To any new parents of a Down's syndrome child, I cannot promise you that after coming to terms with the condition you will have happy and fulfilled lives. I **can** promise you, though, that from our experience and that of others we know, that you will definitely have happy and fulfilled lives. Please take heart: the future is brighter than ever for children with Down's syndrome and there are many parents who have had the same concerns which you now have.

Down's syndrome (DS):

Down syndrome (DS) or **Down's syndrome**, also known as **trisomy 21**, is a genetic disorder caused by the presence of all or part of a third copy of chromosome 21. Down syndrome is the most common chromosome abnormality in humans. It is typically associated with a delay in cognitive ability (mental retardation, or MR) and physical growth, and a particular set of facial characteristics. The average IQ of young adults with Down syndrome is around 50, whereas young adults without the condition typically have an IQ of 100. (MR has historically been defined as an IQ below 70.) A large proportion of individuals with Down syndrome have a severe degree of intellectual disability.

For every thousand babies born, one will have Down's syndrome.

About 750 babies with Down's syndrome are born in the UK each year.

Down's syndrome affects people of all ages, races, religious and economic situations. It is more commonly seen in older mothers aged thirty-seven and above.

Introduction

This book has a fourfold purpose:

1. To give comfort and support for anybody who finds themselves in a similar situation. I hope to make you laugh at times, for, as the cliché goes, laughter is the best medicine. You will probably cry, too. Not that I want to make you sad, but inevitably there are ups and downs in everybody's life, and crying does bring some relief. Although I want to offer support, I do believe in being truthful and not hiding the downside. In short, I aim to cover the good, the bad and the ugly.

2. It is therapeutic for me to write our family story, documenting our thoughts and feelings and reflecting over the years. We were not the first parents to deliver a baby with Down's syndrome, and sadly, will not be the last.

3. I hope it is an enlightening read for anyone, with or without children, especially those lucky enough to have 'typical' children. I use the word 'typical', because I hate to say 'normal', meaning our son is abnormal, but all children are wonderful gifts, so I do not mean to offend anyone. I may use the word 'normal' throughout the book, although I am not keen on it.

4. I hope it is of interest and help to healthcare and other professionals who come across Down's syndrome in their working life. It may help their interactions with parents.

I like to believe that in most cases friends and family do not mean to say hurtful things. I know how easy it is to blurt out some well-meaning thoughts and instantly regret it, so if you are a parent of a Down's syndrome child, be prepared for some jaw-dropping comments by friends, family, acquaintances and random people in the street. If possible, smile inwardly and don't be upset. They have no idea how hurt and shocked you may be feeling and I am sure they are unaware of their unwelcome words.

I cannot begin to explain the enormity of our devastation. There is no doubt that to deliver a special needs baby is absolutely shattering, life-changing, and it was for us the most shocking and sad experience we had ever encountered. The first reaction was disbelief: there must be a mistake. We were devastated and totally numb. To us, it was an enormous tragedy. My husband, Simon, summed it up by saying we would not have felt any worse if our baby had died. We were mourning the loss of our anticipated and hoped-for healthy baby.

I do not mean to offend any friends or family who may recognise their comments captured in this book, but I think I should record them to help other parents cope, laugh or just to realise they are not alone. It may also help professionals to think carefully about their choice of words.

People often say, '*They* love music,' or '*They* are loving,' about Down's syndrome people. This really is upsetting, because the pronoun 'they' is like segregating 'them' from 'us', as if 'they' are aliens of some kind. However, I have sometimes written 'they' in this context in this book, simply to explain a point. Please forgive me; I do not normally say it.

Since writing this, the new royal baby, Prince George of Cambridge, has been born. The world is full of excitement for our future king. Whilst Kate was in labour, everybody waited with bated breath. Our baby was no less special to us. Thank goodness that the prince is chromosomally typical, but imagine the shock if he hadn't been. Prince William said that they could not be happier, and I know Simon and I would have said the same, if our darling Alex had been born as expected.

In the beginning…

Chapter 1

Alison and Simon

Alison

I was born the youngest daughter to my parents, Vin and Phyll Morgan-Jones. I had two older sisters, Wendy and Diane. Post-war, times were hard and many parents struggled to provide for their children. Our home was full of love and support, and I would say we had a very privileged upbringing and happy childhoods.

We were encouraged to work hard and aim high for our future. Our father was an adorable, kind, generous man, and everybody was extremely fond of him. He worked much longer hours than most to build up his practice, so he was not around much in the daytime or early evenings, which meant that our mother was the one to discipline us. Our mother is a lovely woman, too, but it was Mum who had to bring us up and consequently she was, by necessity, quite strict.

We had a childless aunt, Aunty Megs, who we were extremely fond of and saw regularly. Aunty Megs was like a second mum, and she really adored us and spoilt us.

I loved playing with dolls, and had dolls' prams, pushchair, cradle and many other girlie toys. I often pushed my dolls' pram around the local roads, even at age twelve, when many girls were growing up very quickly. I sometimes put on my mother's high-heeled shoes and her bra. I stuffed an apple into each bra cup and put our kittens or a doll in my substantial 1960s dolls' pram—not far short of pram sizes today—for these walks. People would stare with happy anticipation into the pram, expecting to see a baby, and then looked perplexed to see the kittens or doll. I always knew I wanted to be a mother one day. In contrast, one of my sisters liked train sets and cars.

We three girls were given a choice as to whether we went to boarding school or not for our secondary education. This was typical of my parents, wanting the best for us but not wanting to force us into anything we were not happy with. Wendy and I wanted to go to boarding school, but Diane elected to stay at home.

I had read many Enid Blyton books about the fun at boarding schools, and I had heard Wendy's tales, so I was excited to go. The reality was that boarding school was rarely as much fun as portrayed by Enid Blyton. There were limitations on bathing. From memory, this was only three times a week and only on certain days, and we could only wash our hair fortnightly. This was partly a sign of the times but also reflects the harsh school rules as to where and when you were allowed to talk, and with strict 'lights out at 9pm' bedtime rules. We used to listen to our radios quietly under the bed clothes after lights out. One night, the housemistress came in, and through fear, I accidentally turned my radio volume UP rather than down. Needless to say, our housemistress heard it and confiscated my radio for a few weeks. We were only allowed sweets on Wednesdays and Sundays. One 'non-sweet' day, a friend offered me a juicy sweet. Whilst enjoying it, I casually asked her how she managed to get sweets from the locked cupboard and hide them. 'Oh,' she said, 'it was easy. I put them in my knickers.' The sweet suddenly tasted less palatable.

Sports were compulsory twice a day, too, but I made very good friends and had fun, although I did miss my parents. Aunty Megs had also gone to this school, Howell's School, Llandaff, in Cardiff. This was appropriate as we were Welsh. I think boarding school made us very independent and grown-up in early adolescence, since we had to cope with school work, friendships and associated problems without seeing our parents often.

I stayed at Howell's School until I did my 'O' levels at sixteen. I told my parents that I would prefer to go to a day school for my 'A' levels, since I missed them and wanted more of a social life at weekends. So I went to Harrow County School for girls and luckily I soon made some very good new friends.

We used to go out at weekends, shopping and mixing with boys. We loved listening to the Beatles, Rolling Stones and others, and having giggly sleepovers. My father discouraged us from taking a Saturday job, since he did not want this to interfere with our studies, but I did take holiday jobs, like delivering the Christmas post, which was great fun, after the shock of getting up so early. Mum drove me in her dressing-gown to the sorting office about six in the morning, hoping the car would not break down.

I had always wanted to study medicine. I may not have succeeded however hard I worked, but I know I did not work hard enough at school and consequently I did not achieve good enough grades for medical school. Oscar Wilde said that youth is wasted on the young, and this was certainly true for me and schooling, despite encouragement and help from my parents.

After my 'A' levels, I was not sure what path to take, so I started a temporary job with a large pharmaceutical company, then called Glaxo Research, in the Clinical Trials laboratory. The staff were really welcoming and kind. I fitted in very well, and enjoyed earning money. The Director tried to persuade me to go back and study full time, for my sake, but rightly or wrongly, I stayed with the company, getting a permanent position, learning on the job, and I went to Kingsway Princeton College in London, part-time, to study pharmacology, pharmaceutics and dispensing. I passed all the exams with distinction and enjoyed working very much, especially as I was living at home. Although I saved a bit, I loved shopping in Oxford Street for clothes, spending my own money, and I went to Majorca with a girlfriend, also funded by me.

I actually ended up working for the same company for forty-two years, in a number of different roles, so I do not think it was a bad decision made in youth. I had opportunities to travel for work, including to Mumbai, America and Paris. It gave me great pleasure that I succeeded professionally and personally, gaining a senior position in my field, whilst raising a family.

Simon

Simon had a similarly privileged upbringing to mine, with warm, loving parents. He had an older and younger sister and, being the only boy, sandwiched between two girls, I am sure he felt a bit special. Simon was always extremely practical, dismantling his Dinky cars and tyres, building model planes and making home-made swings and play tunnels in the garden. He even built a bicycle and a scooter from parts he found, acquired or bought. Simon is very good at mathematics and he has an IQ higher than most, as his mother has told me. He did actually have it tested as a young boy, I am assured.

Simon went to prep school and then an independent senior school in West London, after which he studied surveying in London. He went into business with his father, surveying, dealing with property maintenance and building. He later branched out alone.

Marriage and the early years

Simon and I met in our teens, through a mutual friend, and we became teenage sweethearts and fell in love. We met at a party and felt instant attraction for each other. Simon had light blond hair, blue eyes and cheeky smile. He loved old cars and was gifted with engineering and mechanical abilities even building a hot-rod car. We enjoyed our dates, at weekends since we were both at school. We enjoyed the cinema, car shows and drag racing. He proposed to me on Valentine's Day when I was twenty-one, and I of course said yes. I remember how exciting it was. He sent me a Valentine card in which he had written, 'I will send you Valentine cards until we are married, but I am buggered if I will after that!' Later on, he said,' Will you marry me?' (By the way, we do still send Valentine cards.)

He also asked my father's permission to marry me. I remember clearly, Simon was waiting for my parents to return from a restaurant to ask my father and wanted both parents present. As soon as they came home, Dad said, 'I am just going to take the dog for a walk,' so we had to wait a bit longer. I knew Simon and I were meant to be, and that we would be really good together and it was all very magical. It was also nice that both our parents were similar people. It is not a necessity, of course, but we liked the fact they began socialising together. We got married in August 1974, after our exams were over. We were extremely lucky as we had jobs, a house, youth, good health and, above all else, love. Like many of our friends, we felt we were a golden couple, since we had everything going for us. I was only twenty-three years old.

Simon and Alison's wedding

My sister had a broken marriage and I ached for her. I realised how fortunate we were.

Soon after our marriage, whilst driving to work, I observed a group of perhaps five young adults waiting for a bus. I noticed them immediately. I hate to say it, but they stood out. They were all large, strangely dressed and had pudding basin haircuts. They played on my mind: they all had Down's syndrome. In truth, I did not like seeing them and they were there every day for some time after. I could not get their images out of my head and I was glad they were not part of my life.

I knew very little about Down's syndrome. A school friend had a sister with Down's syndrome, called Angie, and I was aware that Angie did not talk very clearly and she had a really husky voice and unusual facial characteristics. I hate myself saying all this, but it is the truth, and that is what this book is about, how the human psyche and maternal instinct cope with adversity. I mentioned to my father, in extreme ignorance, how I regularly saw the group of young 'mongols', and how it upset me. He immediately reprimanded me. 'Please do not call them mongols. It is called 'Down's syndrome', a genetic disorder with an extra chromosome 21. They cannot help it and deserve respect. I have a very nice boy in my practice with this condition.' I never used the word 'mongol' again. I had not realised it was a colloquial word for 'Down's syndrome', since I had read the word in text books whilst studying Biology at school. Also, the widely-respected and highly-acclaimed paediatrician Hugh Jolly uses the term in his original publication and in the 1974 re-print of his book, 'Diseases of Children'.

I was surprised at my father's reaction, as I had no idea I was being disrespectful and derogatory. The memory of his reprimand has stayed with me to this day.

I believe in fate, uncanny situations and how things happen for a reason, and so I often wonder, since Alex's birth, if it was mapped out that Simon and I would have a Down's syndrome child, and that somehow, seeing that group of young adults was a 'view' of the future. I often ponder if it was pure coincidence or not, since many people never come across 'Down's syndrome.' Also, Simon helped out with disabled young teenagers as part of a help-the-community scheme whilst at school. He has since told me, after Alex's birth, that he always knew we would have either no children, or a disabled child. He said that he often felt psychic, in that he had predicted one or two things which happened; good things, fortunately. This was news to me as he had not discussed this before. I remember telling him when I travelled to Mumbai for work, fairly recently, that I worried I was not coming back. I think I was just over-anxious about leaving Simon and the children during their last school year. Simon said, 'Oh, don't worry about that. I am sure you will be back, I haven't had any premonitions that you will come to any harm, so you will be OK.' Since he had had no untoward previsions, this guaranteed that I would be OK. Fortunately, back I came.

We had a happy marriage, working hard and renovating our house. We had many friends who we saw regularly, had people for dinner and saved hard for nice holidays, including America and touring around Europe. We knew we were lucky and although we may sound spoilt, we worked hard for it. We knew we wanted children, but not too early in the marriage, because a mortgage is a pretty safe contraceptive, and also we were very young.

After about five years of marriage, we started to discuss children. Both my older sisters had two children each, and one of Simon's sisters had a daughter. We were very fond of our nephews and nieces. We babysat for Ben and Tom, our two nephews living nearby, and if something of theirs broke, they would come around to our house and ask Simon to mend it, knowing of his reputation for fixing things, so we felt very close.

I doubted we would conceive straight away, I had read a lot about fertility problems and I knew that one in seven couples may have some difficulty in conceiving. Of course, I also read articles like 'I got drunk at a party, didn't mean to… And now I'm pregnant.' In fact, one of our friends told us, 'I can't believe how easy it is to conceive; it happened first time we tried.' So, hoping for the best but slightly prepared, we stopped birth control and relaxed. Suffice it to say, there was no conception in year one. I am normally optimistic, but I just knew we were going to have problems; after all, if we were both 'normal' with respect to reproduction and fertility, something would have happened in that first year. We were fairly upbeat about it, but after discussions with my GP, we pursued help under a really nice and friendly gynaecologist and obstetrician, Mr Fisher at Northwick Park Hospital.

With infertility, the man is usually tested first, since it is quick, easy and inexpensive to determine if his sperm are live and adequate. The problem for women is that there are many more tests and procedures, which can take quite some time, especially as some of these are invasive, necessitating time off work, which is awkward, with well-meaning colleagues wondering/asking about the absences, not to mention being able to get your job done. Some of the tests can only be done at certain times of the month, for example, mid-cycle or just after menstruation. During one assessment Mr Fisher wanted to give me hormone injections, but a strict regime is necessary, starting on Day One of a new menstrual cycle. I regularly phoned the hospital's dedicated secretary on this day to hear her say, 'Sorry, Mr Fisher is not available for this cycle,' which meant waiting a whole month before being able to phone her again, possibly to hear the same words. I felt that this person told me with unsympathetic malicious delight, since I detected glee in her voice when she said that I would have to wait another month.

Waiting another month was pure hell, since time was ticking away, and another month's wait seemed an eternity. Perhaps we should have pursued some private treatment, but because it is such a delicate and sensitive issue, we remained under Mr Fisher, especially as we had a very good rapport with him. I later found out that the dedicated secretary was also having fertility problems, and I suppose she was not interested in helping us, and seemed quite happy that we had to wait yet another month, each time we rang.

We managed to see Mr Fisher after missing about four cycles. Four months is an awfully long time when trying to become pregnant. After all the initial tests, including urine, blood, scans and physical examinations, Mr Fisher wanted me to have a laparoscopy (see Reference 2) to check my 'insides'. After all these tests and procedures, he concluded that my fallopian tubes were not blocked, but kinked, and my womb was severely retroverted, and although some gynaecologists would say this should not impede conception, considering we had by then tried to conceive for about two years, he suggested he should write to the late Mr Steptoe at Bourn Hall, Cambridge, to investigate *in vitro* fertilisation (IVF. See Reference 1). This was pretty upsetting, since we knew it took time, meant more time off work, cost a lot of money and there was a fairly low success rate. However, I do not give up easily.

There is a short waiting list for IVF, so all in all, about four years had passed from our initial attempts to conceive and our first 'journey' for IVF at Bourn Hall Clinic. Needless to say, during that time, although we had remained strong and committed as a couple, we had experienced many friends, family and acquaintances conceiving and producing beautiful babies, so with time it became harder to cope with, especially as I was not getting younger. I could tell that family and friends were wondering why we had not conceived and some asked if we were going to have children, which was very painful.

IVF is an exciting but emotional and stressful process. All clinics differ in their procedures, but in those days at Bourn Hall, it was done in this way:

After an initial assessment and referral from a gynaecologist, the patient, i.e. infertile couple, telephones the clinic on Day One of a new menstrual cycle. With bated breath, you wait to hear if the clinic has space for you that month. I was lucky, and was never turned away for another month. You are invited to attend on a certain day of your cycle, as a residential patient. The clinic is in a palatial Jacobean building, with beautiful décor and glorious grounds.

The exciting part is, at last, hopefully becoming pregnant. The emotional part is going through it, meeting some people who are back after previous attempts, some having been successful, most of them not…

From the moment you arrive, all urine must be passed at designated times only, into a named collecting vessel. The urine is then analysed at regular intervals to assess one's hormone levels. Regular hormone injections are administered to make the ovaries produce more eggs for fertilisation with, in most cases, the husband's sperm. For IVF, it is desirable to produce a few eggs, to increase the chances of the eggs fertilising into embryos, and so having more embryos for subsequent implantation into the mother's womb. During the urine analysis, the fertility expert decides when the hormone levels are right, indicating the ovarian eggs are almost ready for releasing from the ovary for the woman to undergo a laparoscopy, under a light general anaesthetic, to remove as many as 'ripened' eggs as appropriate. Laparoscopy can be used for many purposes, but it is used for ovarian egg retrieval for IVF.

In the normal female monthly cycle, described very simply, usually a single egg is ripened and released from the ovary at ovulation into the fallopian tube. It is wafted down the fallopian tube into the womb and, if it meets a sperm in the womb, with luck it will be fertilised to become an embryo and grow to be a healthy baby, embedded in the womb.

For IVF, the fertility specialist relies on very exact science and arranges the laparoscopy for ovarian egg retrieval just before the egg(s) are released from the ovary. Too soon and the eggs will be immature for fertilisation, too late and the ovary will have released them and they will not be retrievable, so timing is absolutely critical.

These eggs are mixed with the sperm and closely watched by the embryologist. If any eggs are fertilised, after being kept in special conditions, the embryologist decides which eggs should be implanted in the woman, and which, if any, can be frozen for subsequent use. This usually takes about three days, and it gives the woman time to recover from the laparoscopy which is quite painful, because the CO_2 causes pain until it is expelled from the body. It is usually decided between the prospective parents and the clinic staff that it is advisable to replace three embryos, if available. Any more could be harmful to the mother if all are implanted and any fewer reduces the chances of at least one implanting and producing a pregnancy.

If more than three embryos are created, it is usual to have them frozen for subsequent use. Sometimes they do not freeze, or sometimes they freeze but do not thaw as viable embryos, so the uncertainty makes for a very stressful and difficult process.

For the woman, the timing is very exciting, knowing she has eggs for harvesting. She has after all been resting and chatting with her new friends, eating well and waiting for 'D' Day. For the man, it can be stressful, knowing he has to be on time, drop everything, leave work and perform by getting his sperm into a jar.

All the women spoke excitedly about having your very own embryos implanted after the IVF cycle. After all, with luck, this is the day you could become pregnant. You are advised to prepare for it by wearing a new, special nightie, doing your hair and make-up as if you were going on a date, and remembering your perfume, nail varnish or whatever you like to use to make you feel good. The feel-good factor is very important psychologically. Scientifically it may not affect the chances of the embryo implanting, but you are clutching at straws to be one of the lucky ones. You are given a time to be ready, and it is always the afternoon or early evening. The special operating theatre has soft lighting, quiet music is playing and there are scenes from idyllic sandy beaches on the walls. The atmosphere is calm and the staff are relaxed and happy. The prospective mother feels amazing, since she has live embryos to be placed in her womb. This procedure takes a very short time, and then you are wheeled back to your bed, where you stay put all evening and night. Tea and sandwiches are brought to you and all your clinic friends visit you to share your hopes. You are hoping with all your heart that at least one of your embryos will divide and implant into your womb. You are euphoric with delight and hope.

The women used to say how the embryologist can choose the 'best' healthy embryos, and how they would be perfect. I later realised after Alex's birth that any screening of the embryos back then could not include chromosomal factors, and people saying 'only perfect embryos are chosen' was a rumour amongst the patients, desperate for a healthy baby. This reflects the terrible sadness of infertility and the desperation with which we wanted to believe that this was true. This belief compounded our shock at learning that Alex had Down's syndrome.

Reference 1

In vitro **fertilisation** (**IVF**) is a process by which an egg is fertilised by sperm outside the body: *in vitro*. IVF is a major treatment for infertility when other methods of assisted reproductive technology have failed. The process involves monitoring a woman's ovulatory process, removing ovum or ova (egg or eggs) from the woman's ovaries and letting sperm fertilise them in a fluid medium in a laboratory. When a woman's natural cycle is monitored to collect a naturally selected ovum (egg) for fertilisation, it is known as natural cycle IVF. The fertilised egg (zygote) is then transferred to the patient's uterus with the intention of establishing a successful pregnancy. The first successful birth of a "test tube baby", Louise Brown, occurred in 1978. Louise Brown was born as a result of natural cycle IVF.

Reference 2-laparoscopy

Laparoscopic surgery, often called keyhole surgery, is minimally invasive, operations in the abdomen being performed through small incisions. The abdomen is usually insufflated, or essentially blown up like a balloon, with carbon dioxide (CO_2) gas. This elevates the abdominal wall above the internal organs like a dome to create a working and viewing space. CO_2 is used because it is common to the human body and can be absorbed by tissue and removed by the respiratory system.

Bourn Hall Clinic is amazing. We met so many nice, but unlucky people having the same problems as us, but it is very encouraging and therapeutic to share stories and gonad histories. I found arriving at Bourn Hall quite euphoric. I knew we had a journey to make, but it was a step nearer to our goal.

Bourn Hall and similar organisations must be the only places where you discuss sperm counts and fallopian tubes with virtual strangers without any embarrassment whatsoever. Indeed, it is commonplace to do so, since we all had the same objective. These conversations usually take place over delicious dinners in the clinic dining room. One minute you may say, 'Please can you pass the mayonnaise,' and then ask an acquaintance how many of their eggs were retrieved for fertilising during the IVF process.

I remember meeting one woman at Bourn Hall who had had an abortion as a teenager, and now was unable to conceive naturally. It was sad to see how she berated herself.

After four attempts at IVF, I was not pregnant. Each time the clinic managed to retrieve about four of my eggs, fertilise them with Simon's sperm and replace three embryos at a suitable time. But each time, the embryos failed to implant. I cannot put into words how awful that is, I really cannot. Your hopes are taken up sky high, you are on cloud nine hoping and praying…and then you menstruate. This is an almighty slap in the face and I cannot overemphasise the utmost feeling of despair and desperation.

Also each time the fourth embryo was frozen, it did not freeze properly, so it could not be used.

I tried not to dwell on the potential babies we had created, but I did wonder what sex they would have been, what they would have looked like and what people they may have become. Would we ever be parents?

On one occasion when I returned to work after a failed IVF attempt, I was particularly dreading seeing my friends and colleagues. I was feeling very low but not wanting to show this. I had not been back more than thirty minutes when my friend Sally came to see me and ecstatically said, 'Hi, Ali, guess what, I am pregnant!' I remember so well how I felt. Of course I was delighted for Sally, but I wanted to cry so much. Why did I have to hear this news so soon after returning to work? Why was this happening to me? What had I done to deserve this? Words cannot describe the sadness and desolation that I felt.

I actually met Lesley Brown, who was the mother of the world's first test tube baby, Louise Brown, at Bourn Hall Clinic, who was there hoping for a second baby. Lesley did produce a second daughter by IVF, Natalie, but I am not sure if it was that or a subsequent attempt where Natalie was created. Lesley was in my room/ward and it was wonderful to meet her and so encouraging for all of us lucky enough to meet her.

On our fifth attempt at IVF, which was in 1986, two years after we had started treatment at Bourn Hall, I told Simon and my sister, 'I can't do this again, after this fifth attempt, I just can't.' Taking time off work and saying it was for confidential medical reasons, as if they would not know, the emotional strain, the cost and fibbing to friends and family about where I was for many days at a time were taking their toll. Also, Simon had to come at the drop of a hat, literally, if you forgive me for being crude, since he had to arrive on a certain day, at short notice, to produce his sperm in a jar, at a certain time so that the scientists could attempt to fertilise my egg(s) with the sperm, in a petri dish actually, and not a test tube.

I think I built a shell around myself and used to pretend to be flippant about babies, saying we didn't want them, because the last thing you want is sympathy or people asking, 'No sign of a baby yet, then?' Also, it may be impossible to believe but it seemed that all around us, friends and family were conceiving constantly. It seemed that each time our IVF attempts failed, someone close announced pregnancy, unaware that to us it was a massive kick in the teeth. We had to smile and hide our grief, uttering 'Congratulations' with aching hearts. It was not their fault we could not conceive. I was not jealous they were pregnant, but extremely envious. Wherever we went, I was so aware of all the seemingly numerous babies in prams, or kept seeing countless television adverts for baby products, starring beautiful babies. Returning to work on the days after a failed IVF attempt, when I was always very downhearted, there was usually some news of a pregnancy. My sister and sister-in-law both announced a pregnancy during our desperate years of trying to conceive. It was extremely difficult for us, but we coped. I think because infertility is not an illness *per se*, it is not something you can discuss easily with friends and family. What can they say? I could not stand the thought of friends talking about us, albeit kindly. My parents knew all about Bourn Hall but I did not want to share it with my in-laws, though after about five years of infertility, we thought it was only fair to tell Simon's parents, since they loved him and we knew they would be wondering.

Overall, we just about coped with infertility, as we are a strong couple, but if Simon was a bit low, I convinced myself it was my fault for not conceiving, so I became a bit low, too. After a bad respiratory infection, I had pleurisy, which brought me right down. Not one for self-pity, I soon bounced back fortunately. I remember Simon staring out of the window looking forlorn one day. I asked him what the matter was. He replied, 'It would be different if we had children.' I felt awful.

I do remember saying to him one day, 'You go off while you are still young and find someone who can give you babies.' He said, 'Don't be so ridiculous,' which to me was both hilarious and flattering, although I did really want to hear something such as, 'Oh, don't be silly. It's you I love, with or without children.'

My mother did not cope with it very well, but just as we often do not tend to realise our mothers may be worrying about us taking exams or having a sore throat, I had no idea. My mother-in-law told me that she saw my mother one time when I was at Bourn Hall, and mentioned something about 'poor Ali, and what she is going through', and my mother burst into tears. Poor Mum, she must have found it hard to express her sorrow for us, so I thought she was indifferent to the IVF, but I then realised she was really suffering but did not dare show it. As I am now fortunate enough to be a mother I totally understand.

Chapter 2

The Pregnancy

After about seven years of hoping for a baby, comprised approximately of one year of 'trying', three years of obstetric consultations and three of intermittent IVF cycles, after the fifth attempt at IVF, having said that I couldn't go through it again, EUREKA! After a routine visit to the clinic, now, at age thirty-six, I WAS PREGNANT! We were absolutely overjoyed; words cannot describe our elation. We realised it was early days, and anything could happen, but it was a step further to parenthood that we had not until then experienced.

Then I started slight vaginal bleeding, and naturally I was very worried. I had a scan and examination, and was told everything seemed in order, but I was to have daily progesterone injections for three months. This was a small price to pay, and I was extremely lucky as my father arranged for his nurse to administer the injections until I returned to work and then the company nurse administered them for me. The three months soon passed and all was progressing well.

I loved being pregnant and all the family made a great fuss of me. It was overwhelmingly wonderful looking at babies, and baby clothes in the shops, along with cots and other baby equipment, especially after all the years of waiting and hoping.

It was 1986, and my first scan was carried out at sixteen weeks of the pregnancy, which was the usual practice back then. At the excitement of this first scan at Northwick Park hospital, Mr Fisher attended. As we watched the baby move, he held my hand and had a tear in his eye. It was a wonderful experience. I asked casually if I should have an amniocentesis, (Reference 3) to detect any defects. Mr Fisher said, 'No, no need with respect to your age, since the risk of such defects at your age are small.' Also, he said, my placenta was anterior and an amniocentesis was out of the question, so that was that. There is a risk of miscarriage with the amniocentesis. To miscarry any baby is heart breaking, but to miscarry a baby as much wanted and much waited for as ours would have been catastrophic, especially as we were unlikely to conceive again.

Reference 3

Amniocentesis is a medical procedure used in <u>prenatal diagnosis</u> of <u>chromosomal abnormalities</u> and foetal infections, also for sex determination, in which a small amount of amniotic fluid, which contains foetal tissues, is <u>sampled</u> from the <u>amnion</u> or amniotic sac surrounding a developing <u>foetus</u>, and the foetal DNA is examined for genetic abnormalities.

Chapter 3

The Delivery

Overall my pregnancy proceeded well. I experienced minimal nausea in the early days, and all other routine tests like blood pressure (BP) were normal. We felt extremely happy, excited and blessed. Mr Fisher saw me regularly and I honestly think he was as excited as us. I carried on working until about thirty-four weeks pregnant.

At about thirty-five weeks, Mr Fisher thought I was not gaining enough weight and he felt the baby was small. My parents kindly, and probably desperately, rushed round with steak and other nourishing food, but I knew I had been eating healthily. Mr Fisher said he would like to admit me to hospital for observation. I went to the hospital to stay on a Friday. I had regular fœtal checks and there did not seem to be much concern. The baby's heartbeat was sound. A paediatrician visited me on the following Monday, along with Mr Fisher. The paediatrician sat and talked to me. He said, 'There will be a reason that your baby is small.' I don't think I grasped that he was trying to warn me that there might be something wrong. Mr Fisher, who liked to be jovial, said, 'Better out than in. At thirty-six weeks your baby will do better in an incubator than inside you. You are having a caesarean this afternoon. We do not want you to have an induced 'normal' delivery. It will be too much for the baby.' Naturally, my adrenalin was flowing fast. I rang Simon and then my mother, and burst into tears. I was overwhelmed emotionally and slightly traumatised.

At 4 pm, I was taken down to theatre, followed by my good friend Christine and her two very young children, who had arrived for visiting just as I was about to be wheeled away. Poor Christine, who had struggled to get her two children ready and driven ten miles for visiting, just to wave me off, looked bewildered. That probably applied to both of us. Fortunately, I was able to have an epidural so I could be awake throughout, and Simon was by my side, holding my hand. This was considered an elective caesarean as opposed to an emergency one, since the pregnancy was not felt to be life threatening. Christine had herself had an emergency caesarean, and I think she was assuming I was in the same situation, as I did not really have time to speak properly with her.

Everything seemed to proceed well and we were all chatting away. I only felt the slightest pressure on my abdomen, and absolutely no discomfort. The staff placed a metal contraption over my abdominal area and a green cloth, so I could not see what was going on. At one point, Mr Fisher asked, 'Do you want to see the baby coming out?' to which I replied, 'No, thank you,' but I then realised that he was talking to Simon, and not me. Mr Fisher announced, 'It's a boy!' Suddenly, I felt extremely woozy. Mr Fisher took Simon out of the theatre, not that I was aware of this. He told Simon I had lost a lot of blood and needed a blood transfusion. If the bleeding did not stop within minutes, I would have to lose my womb. Simon remembers thinking that this wouldn't be so bad, since we had a beautiful son. I think I was fairly close to death, actually, and that without an experienced senior obstetrician present, I would almost certainly have been given a hysterectomy.

The bleeding stopped and I remember Mr Fisher saying I was very weak and would have to stay in the delivery suite for the night and have hourly checks for BP and to make sure my wound did not start bleeding again. I was not out of the woods and they hoped to save my womb. Our new son (4lbs 2oz./1.9 kg) was breathing well but would be in the Special Care Baby Unit (SCBU) to be checked over. Also, I was in no fit state to care for him since I could not muster the energy to do so. I was weak and tired and, although I hate to say it, I didn't feel very overjoyed at that moment, in spite of my longed-for motherhood.

I was put in a room of my own and had a bad night. Every hour, the automatic BP machine went 'click, click, click' as it tightened the tourniquet around my arm, took my BP and went 'tick, tick, tick' as it printed out the reading. Then the nurse came to check the readings and look at my bandages to see if there was any bleeding. The urinary catheter pulled uncomfortably between my legs. I knew I was having excellent care, but all these checks meant I could not sleep. Every time I fell asleep, these noises woke me with a start, which made me jump and that made my wound hurt.

Alex in SCBU

Chapter 4

Day 1 of the Rest of Our Lives – The First 25 Years

After a difficult night, I was feeling sorry for myself. I began to reprimand myself for feeling low with these post-operative effects, as we had, after all these years, produced a much wanted and waited-for baby boy.

The SCBU had sent a Polaroid photo down of our son being cuddled by Simon, which was on my bedside unit. I looked at it and was absolutely overjoyed that I was, at last, a mother of a perfect baby boy. Nothing could destroy my happiness. Oh, my God, I thought, we actually have a beautiful baby at last!

Little did I know what was to follow…

I was just starting to feel good mentally; physically I was very uncomfortable, to say the least. Though not wishing to wallow in the post-operative conditions I was suffering, I will just give the facts, since they are relevant to the story.

A nurse came in to introduce herself and do her checks. I cannot pinpoint it, but this nurse made me feel uncomfortable. I felt she looked at me oddly, smiling falsely, or do I mean unkindly? It reminded me of a child at school, telling another child 'teacher wants to see you', knowing the first child is in trouble.

I told the nurse my 'secret' about the childless years of heartache we'd had, and how lucky we were. I picked up the Polaroid photo and said something like, 'Look at my perfect baby—just imagine, he could have had Down's syndrome or something.' Don't ask me why I said that, but the nurse replied, with her false grin, 'They think he has got Down's syndrome.'

Naturally, I felt the uttermost disbelief, numbness and shock that it is possible to feel. I prayed that I was dreaming. I looked at the SCBU photo: impossible. How dare she? Every emotion passed through my mind. She said the paediatrician wanted to see Simon and me later that morning, and promptly left the room. What a bitch. It was as if she had enjoyed bringing me bad news, and she had left me in limbo.

The distress took the form of shock, and I will never, ever, forget how I felt. I know one does not shoot the messenger, but this nurse had an un-endearing expression on her face. *Schadenfreude*, if ever I saw it. The outcome was the same, though, whatever she said or did; we had produced a baby with Down's syndrome.

It's difficult to know if life has ever been the same since, although all new parents could say this, because having a baby is a life-changing experience. Every pregnant woman might occasionally think about the possibility of her unborn child being less than perfect, but I always put it out of my mind, thinking, surely not after all this...

Simon arrived soon after I had heard the worst news of my life, with his camera. He was so elated, proud and happy; everything seemed wonderful to him. He was overjoyed to have a son to help him with the cars. He had no idea what the nurse had said to me. There was no way in the world I could indicate to him what she had suggested. I only told him that the paediatrician wanted to see us, and fortunately he seemed to think this was a matter of course. He was telling me all about the announcement phone calls he had made to family and friends, and how exciting it was, and relaying all sorts of good messages. I just froze, and listened to him without speaking. He said, 'What's wrong?' He thought I would be smiling continuously. I just told him I felt uncomfortable after the monitoring checks I had had during the night.

The paediatrician, unaware the nurse had spilt the beans, had a standard speech for such situations. He said that parents of seemingly 'normal' children do not know how their children will turn out, how they may become drug addicts or criminals. I know he was trying to soften the blow, but it didn't seem apposite, especially when he went on to say that they thought our son had Down's syndrome and not to be unduly worried. They would have to do a blood test to confirm the condition.

It is difficult to describe the shock and despair we felt. Inevitably, you hope the diagnosis is wrong. You think maybe they muddled your baby with someone else's. You are upset, desperate and cannot quite believe it. How can you take it in? After eight years you become pregnant, taken up high in the clouds, only wanting what most people want and many take for granted, although we never did, then are dropped crashing down to earth like that. Was this really happening to us?

Simon initially thought the paediatrician had just come in for a friendly chat and he wanted to spend some time with me and then visit our beautiful baby before going to work, whereas I knew what news was coming.

I glanced at Simon. He looked absolutely shattered. His face was a pale grey colour, and he bit his lip. His eyes seemed wet, but he held the tears back. We hugged each other and I remember saying, 'You won't leave me, will you?' and he replied, 'You won't leave me, will you?' We laugh about it now, but this news was so unexpected and we had no clue how the other was really thinking. With all these mixed emotions, one thing we never felt was bitterness, which just poisons your mind.

We were absolutely devastated. 'What have we done?' we asked ourselves. I had always felt lucky and happy, and this news certainly wiped the smiles off our faces. We were distraught and slightly frightened of our future. *What future?* we wondered. How could we tell our close family, friends and other relatives?

Chapter 5

The Baby – Acceptance

We accepted our baby into our hearts, home and lives instantly. We adored and loved him so much. What we did not easily accept was the Down's syndrome. I knew without asking Simon that he wanted our baby one hundred per cent, but I had to ask him. He was very upset, and replied, 'How could you even think that? We waited all this time, but then send him back because he is not quite right?' He was shocked and I cried.

When Alex was about two or three days old and still in SCBU, the paediatrician announced that Alex definitely had Down's syndrome. Of course, they were 99.9% positive from the start, but they needed the confirmation of the blood test. Because of Alex's size and prematurity, I was not able to hold him properly for a few days, by which time we'd had the confirmation of the Down's syndrome, but I bonded straight away.

It is really lovely to cuddle a smaller than average baby. You have more time watching them grow. I remember one of the nurses telling me this and she was right. To us, he looked so gorgeous and very tiny. To my untrained eye, it was impossible to tell from his features that there was anything wrong. I kept thinking, it's not his fault, he doesn't want to be like this. I think that is what kept me going. The maternal instinct is a wonderful thing. The paediatrician said we could leave our baby behind for fostering or adoption and go home without him ... UNTHINKABLE. We could never leave our flesh and blood behind. Everyone's situation is different so I would not blame other parents who might not want their child, but Simon and I wanted Alex so badly. I remember saying I would far rather have Alex than no baby. In fact, I cried to my mother one evening, saying I did not want Alex to die. Not that there was any reason for him to die, such as health complications. I certainly did not want to give him away, but I wished he didn't have the Down's syndrome.

It is distressing to recall that many years ago, parents of Down's syndrome babies were encouraged to leave their baby in institutions, brandishing them retarded and uneducable. I shudder to think of their care, lack of parental love, and what the parents went through.

I cannot remember who talked about this, definitely not Dr Lieberman, the paediatrician, but one of the doctors even suggested we could perform cosmetic surgery on Alex to make him more 'normal' looking. We cannot imagine ever subjecting him to that. To us it was barbaric and shocking to have suggested it. Alex is our son as he is.

The early days are slightly blurry. Simon and I were no doubt totally shell-shocked. The thought of telling anyone about Alex seemed such an onerous task, I cannot easily explain why. I cannot say I was ashamed, but it was as if I was ashamed. I just did not want to say it, probably because of my ridiculous negative views of Down's syndrome. How could I know otherwise, though? Also, some people said things like, 'Well, you are an elderly mother and Down's syndrome is more common in older mothers.' I know Simon did not blame me in any way, but I think I blamed myself.

If, heaven forbid, our baby had been born ill, I could have told people far more easily. That may sound terrible, but it is the truth.

Many new mothers of Down's syndrome babies feel the same, so if you are a new mother of a Down's syndrome baby, do not be surprised at this. My father came to visit me soon after the unpleasant nurse had mentioned the Down's syndrome to me. He could not understand why I didn't seem elated. I told him I had had a bad night and was just having some post-operative effects. He went to the SCBU, saw our baby, and asked the nurse if the baby had Down's syndrome. He came back to see me and I cried… and that was one of the very few times I saw my darling dad cry, too. It was awful. True to form, my dad was a great source of comfort, support and love. I told Simon not to tell people yet. I wanted to enjoy my visitors and all their congratulatory wishes and show them our darling baby. There seems such a stigma with a disabled child but this was my naive attitude, I know. Visitors came and went, bearing gifts, cards and wonderful messages. Yes, I was living a lie, I just could not bear to tell my close friends and family that I was going through such torment. To me, telling our friends, colleagues and acquaintances about the Down's syndrome seemed as dreadful as if I had to tell them I was going to prison for some petty crime, however crazy that sounds. It is inexplicable, feeling like this, so shameful, but our emotions were in knots.

My friends have since told me that our delay in telling them about the Down's syndrome upset them. They wanted to shake me, with love. They said, 'We are your friends who love you and want to support you. How could you not share this with us, your friends?' I often hid our feelings because you don't want to cry in front of some people, be they friends, relatives or strangers, and sympathy makes it worse. Most people felt upset for us, and would accept Alex, but I also know that others viewed Down's syndrome negatively (who can blame them?) and would tell their young children tactlessly, 'Alex is not normal and he looks different.' I knew our friends' children would need to be told, but there are ways of doing this.

I stayed in hospital a week. The paediatrician told us that during this week that Alex would be taken by ambulance to the world-renowned heart hospital at Harefield in Middlesex for heart checks, when they had a suitable appointment slot. One evening, my mother-in-law, Maggie, visited me. We had not yet told her about the Down's syndrome. She was overjoyed, of course, especially since she had two granddaughters, and now she had a grandson to carry on the family name... All these situations were so traumatic that I cannot begin to describe them properly. Whilst Maggie was there, the paediatrician stuck his head round the door and said, 'Good news! We took the baby to Harefield today and he has no heart defects or other systemic problems commonly seen with Down's children.' I froze. Then I had to explain to Maggie, and, of course, I cried. The 'good health news' announced by the paediatrician was moved to another compartment of my brain at that moment, since I had to discuss Alex and the Down's syndrome with Maggie. This was very awkward for me. Naturally, she was very sympathetic. I felt guilty and upset for not being well enough to accompany our baby in the ambulance, which highlights my feelings and unconditional love for him.

The next day my sister-in-law, Sue, visited. I elatedly walked to the SCBU with her, ready to show her our new baby. I naively thought Sue would not know about the Down's syndrome yet, and I was not ready to tell her. But she said, 'My mother told me about the Down's syndrome.' I froze again, not knowing what to say. Many of us don't like to cry in front of people, so I put on my brave face, albeit with great difficulty.

My lovely obstetrician, Mr Fisher, came to see me soon after the official diagnosis. I could see he was very upset. He said, 'Love your baby, care for him, try not to be over-protective and remember you still have a husband to love and care for. Try to spend time together and have date nights.' Then he produced a second bombshell. He said the delivery had been very difficult, hence my blood loss and blood transfusion. My pregnancy was termed 'anterior saculation', which is apparently quite rare, so I could not read up much about it. It meant Alex was squashed in a corner of my womb, hence his growth slowed *in utero*. He could actually have died if an elective caesarean had not been carried out early. This made it very hard to remove Alex safely and stop the bleeding and not damage my womb irreparably. This was why Simon saw blood all over the operating theatre floor and how I nearly had to have a hysterectomy to save my life from haemorrhaging. As mentioned earlier, I then knew that I and/or Alex could have died, if we had not had such an experienced consultant as dear Mr Fisher. We are so grateful to him, since without him present, a more junior doctor may well have struggled with such a delivery.

Mr Fisher said that however bizarre it seemed after waiting so long for a baby, he was concerned how I was healing internally and therefore it was imperative that Simon and I avoided a highly unlikely but possible conception until he could carry out some tests. He said he had no idea how my womb would heal. He said I may never menstruate again, or I may menstruate and the waste material may not be able to leave my body without obvious health risks and pain. He said to come and see him when I felt ready for the tests, after at least six months, or sooner if I had any bad pains.

The hospital suggested I came home for a few nights before Alex was discharged from the SCBU. It gave Simon and me some time on our own and to get organised, if you can ever be organised with a new baby. Of course this meant I was backwards and forwards to the hospital for feeding times and general care. I did think that I was not supposed to drive soon after a caesarean section, but when I asked my obstetrician, 'Can I drive?' he flippantly retorted, 'If you have got a licence!' So I was able to drive back and forth to hospital daily to see our baby.

Numerous well-wishing cards, gifts and flowers arrived. I kept thinking if only things were different and our baby was as he should be. Just as with sudden unexpected bereavement, we were still numb.

I remember thinking that some of the other cruel occurrences in life, such as redundancy or alcoholism, with luck may go away, or be managed, but with Down's syndrome, there is no going-away. It is there for life, and the future did seem bleak.

Looking back, I think we coped very well. We loved each other and we loved our baby. Also, life with a new baby, especially to an inexperienced, shell-shocked first-time mother, is extremely busy. Alex came home when he was about a week old. We accepted him at once, but I know our cat was not amused, sniffing around the cot in a very suspicious manner.

When I was expecting Alex and had been admitted to hospital before his delivery, a friend of one of my sisters kindly visited me. The friend had always been very nice to me, and said she would like to visit me after the baby was born. I was very happy about that. After Alex's birth, I never heard from her again. I know this was because she did not know what to say or do, but it was very hurtful nevertheless. I have seen her twice in the last ten years at my sister's parties, but we did not discuss children.

I am conscious that I may be writing some things like, 'I did this with Alex', or, 'I thought this', and I can hear Simon saying, when he reads this, 'Why did you write "I" and not "we"'? The fact is, I did not share all my thoughts with Simon; that would not have been fair. He could come home after a difficult day at work or perhaps a good day and I did not want to greet him at the door with 'I feel depressed' or similar statements. Strangely, I did not get depressed, just very down sometimes, but then very easily upbeat again, caring for our gorgeous baby. I did feel 'why us?', since it was so unlikely we could have another baby. My sister Diane offered to carry a baby for us, which was such a kind thought. I held that thought for a long time, which was another reason to be more cheerful.

My brother-in-law, Edwin, said he did not think to have a Down's syndrome child was so terrible, but it is when you first hear it announced, believe me. Mainly, I think, because it is so unexpected, undesired and you do not have a proper understanding of the implications and how life will be. Fear of the unknown is also a massive part. Doesn't everybody want a beautiful, delightful, typical baby to be proud of?

You definitely have some weird thoughts when you have a child with special needs. You wonder how they will be, will they get a job, will they marry, and so on. Mothers do not normally think of things like that when they have just produced a 'normal' typical baby.

There were moments when I was almost suicidal, but these passed instantly. I always thought I would 'leave it behind' if we had a disabled child. How I underestimated the maternal and paternal instincts. We loved Alex more than anything and I knew I would rather have a disabled baby than no baby, but all the same, the pain we felt is indescribable. I would not wish this heartache on my worst enemy. I worried about our family and friends accepting Alex. This was totally unnecessary, but it was on my mind. Nearly everybody we knew was so supportive and loving and kind. In fact, I was surprised and happy, of course, regarding most people's reactions. I do remember thinking, I won't be able to go to the shopping mall again, and ridiculous things like that. I cannot remember why I thought that about the shopping mall; I think I just felt our lives had changed irrevocably.

I thought back to being a little girl, and pushing the kittens in my dolls' pram, and people's faces when they had expected to see a baby in the pram. I imagined I would get similar reactions to people looking in my pram and seeing Alex and the Down's syndrome characteristics, but fortunately, I was wrong.

It's a hard world out there and you need your faculties. It may be shallow, but most of us are vain and want to look nice and I abhor the facial characteristics associated with people with Down's syndrome, for their sake. Very few Down's syndrome babies abort naturally, so God/Nature regards them as compatible with life.

Most days were quite normal, or as normal as any day is with a new baby. Alex was quite a good baby, and feeding every three or four hours was very time-consuming, along with visits to the clinic/health visitor for weighing and general health checks. We had a really supportive health visitor called Linda, and I met many friends at the clinic. We also went to the paediatrician and physiotherapist fairly often and our parents, sisters and friends were marvellous in helping out, phoning and calling in and generally keeping in close contact. Occasionally I felt desolate, but I always had this tiny lovely baby, our own flesh and blood, to care for, though I worried about the future. I didn't want to face up to Alex's future, not wanting to envisage the adult Down's. To us, Alex was our baby without any label of 'Down's syndrome'. Every so often there was the cruel reminder of the syndrome and I felt really sad. Alex gave wonderful smiles, and my mother-in-law remarked how lovingly he looked at me. Also I realised that with any luck that Alex would not suffer. He was medically fit, very happy and he probably wouldn't know he was different.

The paediatrician told us that if you have a disabled child, Down's syndrome is one of the best disabilities to have. It may be something you don't at the time want to hear, but now I really believe it is true. In most cases, children like Alex will walk, talk, eat, read, write, swim and do many other things, whereas other children with different conditions may not be able to. Also, looking different, as children with Down's syndrome do, means that people will see the disability and will understand/expect if the child's behaviour is backward. I have met mothers of children who look completely typical but have 'problems' and who say it is very hard because people cannot understand why their children are behaving awkwardly and they get stared at or teased. How cruel and hard life can be if you are less than perfect—an early lesson we soon learnt.

Simon says he remembers thinking that maybe we should sell our home and disappear to the wilds of Scotland, away from the world we knew. This is how desperate people at a low ebb consider various possibilities.

We were very lucky with the support and help offered to us in the early days. Of course, I just wanted to enjoy our new baby without the reminder of the Down's syndrome from the many hospital appointments, but one should not look a gift horse in the mouth. We were offered physiotherapy, then speech therapy and occupational therapy later, and swimming when Alex was a few months old. I know the staff meant well, but sometimes it was hard. The physiotherapist wanted Alex to stretch over a large ball to strengthen his muscles and aid stability, and of course he cried as it must have been uncomfortable. I hated him crying, naturally, so I came home in tears, too. Many sessions were very positive, though, and all the staff were extremely kind and caring, and it was not their fault if sometimes I thought, please, just leave us alone. I don't want weekly physiotherapy and other sessions, I just want to care for my baby, but I could not be selfish when it was for Alex's benefit.

One of the speech therapists had such a strong Swedish accent that it was quite comical to hear her asking Alex to repeat her words. She asked Alex about clothes you put on to go out in the winter. She wanted him to say 'glove', but with her strong accent she was asking Alex to say 'gloorve' and 'scorrrrf'.

I remember asking one paediatrician that whilst we knew Down's syndrome meant having a small brain, but if Alex had been destined to be bright without the extra chromosome, could it be expected that he may be fairly bright, within the spectrum of Down's syndrome? This of course was my usual optimistic side showing. The answer put me in my place. It was 'Let's call a spade, a spade here.' ... I will not say any more about this.

I was never down for long. Life was too busy and I often took Alex to a shopping mall! There were feeding rooms and pushchair/pram access was easy. My mother often came and we had happy days out.

One day my sister Wendy phoned to see how we were. I was feeling low, and I said, 'Sh*t a brick, how did we get a Down's syndrome baby? What dreadful luck.' This was not my usual choice of words and I was crying. Wendy said, 'I'm coming over,' which was so good of her since it was an hour's drive and she had two boys and a husband to look after. When she arrived I was feeling much better. A good cry always helps.

I met many friendly expectant mothers at the antenatal clinics. In one particular group there were five of us, all due at a similar time. Alex arrived first, so we were home and settling in to our new life before the other four babies arrived. Alex and I attended a session while the other mums were waiting for their new arrivals. I just could not tell them about Alex's condition. He slept through the meeting and they all drooled over him. Soon after, the others produced their babies. One of them, Ann, phoned to say, 'I had a girl, Rhianna.' Ann sounded really cheerful, and said, 'Rhianna came out blue, but hopefully everything is OK.' In my extreme ignorance, I thought, if only Alex had been a bit blue, not understanding the seriousness. It turned out that poor little beautiful Rhianna was severely disabled with profound cerebral palsy. Down's syndrome is a far less disabling disability. Rhianna was having epileptic fits; she could not suck easily, or move. She cried most of the time and her parents soon realised she would never walk, talk or move. It was absolutely heart breaking. Rhianna needed almost round-the-clock care. I felt so bad about all our misgivings about Alex. Ann was a health visitor, so when I confided to her that Alex had Down's syndrome, she nodded and said, 'I know, I could tell.' I should not have been surprised, Ann had an experienced eye; Alex to us was our beautiful baby.

*

Sadly, Rhianna died aged ten of a severe viral infection. Soon after, her father, Peter, also died. Both Ann and Peter had been wonderful parents, who had been as shell-shocked as we were. Peter had started drinking with all the stress and, devastatingly, died. Stories like that put me in my place. What did we have to complain about?

Once Peter had said, 'Last night when Rhianna was crying, I thought, this is a life sentence, but five minutes later, she was asleep, and everything was OK again.'

Chapter 6

Getting On With Life Ahead

The hospital referred us to a geneticist. Since Down's syndrome is a genetic accident, I thought lightning will not strike twice. However, the geneticist said since we had had one baby with a genetic flaw, we would be quite likely to have another, possibly Edwards' syndrome or Turner syndrome, if we were lucky enough to conceive again. Since Alex was still very new, and we were not considering more children at that stage, I put it to the back of my mind.

I did not want to return to work, I just did not want to leave our gorgeous baby, but there were financial considerations, so I went to see our department head, dear Clive, when Alex was about five months old. I felt sick and uncomfortable going in to my department. I had to tell my friends and colleagues about Alex. It was heart-wrenching; I felt sad, embarrassed and emotional. It is difficult to explain the embarrassment. I think it was because there is such a stigma about what we now call learning disability problems which were then known as mental handicap. People often feel the same about saying their relative has schizophrenia, as opposed to, say, heart failure. I felt as bad as I would if I was telling them I had committed a terrible crime. The last thing you want is sympathy and everybody talking about you.

A well-meaning colleague told me she knew an adult Down's syndrome girl. Naturally, I wanted to know the girl's capabilities, so I asked about this. My friend replied, 'She can lay the table.' I was devastated and upset, and livid with myself for having asked the question. How degrading is that? Actually, I think Alex learnt to lay the table when he was about ten, maybe younger.

Clive and my manager, Geoff, sadly both passed away now, very prematurely, were so supportive and kind. I asked if I could return for three days a week, since I had extra appointments for Alex. Clive negotiated with Human Resources and I returned to work when Alex was about six months old, on January 19th. This date proved to be uncannily apt.

I was extremely lucky with childcare arrangements. My mother and mother-in-law had Alex one day a week each, and we had a family friend, Michelle, who couldn't wait to nanny for us. The journey on my first day back was awful. Leaving Alex behind, I felt very anxious and upset. Fortunately, I worked with so many great people that returning to work was wonderful, so much better than I could ever have imagined. I loved being 'Alison Lane' again, the interactions with colleagues, working and galvanising myself back into action to be dressed, not covered in burp milk and ready to face the world, not to mention earning some money again.

This was a very happy period for us. Alex thrived, he was sleeping at night and such a good happy baby, and how we loved him. And we had no child-care worries.

I remember a dear friend, Ingrid, coming to visit. I had met Ingrid at Bourn Hall and she had been very lucky in conceiving her son, Tom, by IVF, at the same time as us. Tom was a gorgeous healthy baby. I told Ingrid how I felt and she asked if we had regretted our IVF, which was a fair question. I emphatically said, 'Oh no.' Whilst we obviously would have preferred that Alex did not have Down's syndrome, we had no regrets and could not imagine life without him.

We also had great support from a programme called Portage, where a person visits you in your own home weekly. Portage is described as 'a home-visiting educational service for pre-school children with additional support needs and their families.' Our Portage worker, Helen, became a great friend and we still meet up now. Helen would advise about encouraging Alex to move towards toys, feed himself, crawl and generally progress in everyday tasks. Helen had four children, her youngest having Down's syndrome.

When Alex was five months old, we decided to take him on holiday to Spain. I was feeding him myself and he was a very good baby, so we knew it would be relatively easy to take him on an aeroplane. The grandmothers seemed alarmed, saying, 'Where are you going to put the baby?' We laughed at this, and wanted to tease them by saying, 'In the hold, of course,' but thought better of it. My mother came and looked after Alex all day before we travelled, so I could pack. We had to leave about 5 am and travel to the airport. We had not listened to the news. It did seem quite cold and windy, but it was October. We couldn't understand why a tree had blown across the main road. Undeterred, we turned around and went on a different road. On arrival at the airport on October 16th 1987, we learnt there had been a terrible hurricane, with vast damage in the South of England. Trust us to be going on holiday then!

Our plane was not able to take off from Luton Airport, so we had to be transferred to Gatwick by coach and fly from there. We eventually arrived in Spain about five in the afternoon. Alex was as good as gold. This was a perfect age to take a baby away since he was not mobile and I had milk ready for him 'on tap'. The hurricane gave the grandmothers some worry, but everything was fine for the flight and onward journey to our hotel. I think Alex had reacted to something I had eaten which affected my milk, since he made the loudest windy noises I had ever heard, sitting near a businessman on the plane. I refrained from saying 'sorry', in case he thought I had made the noises.

Our hotel was really nice, and a cot was waiting for Alex. He slept so well, and we had leisurely breakfasts in bed each morning, so we could feed him without having to rush to the dining-room for breakfast. The holiday was great and we met some nice people who drooled over Alex. I did not mention the Down's syndrome, I felt there was no need. Probably many people guessed, but we enjoyed them asking about our baby and pretending everything was just fine.

Christmas soon came, and everybody spoilt Alex. Many times we thought 'if only…', but we had accepted Alex, and largely got on with it. His smiles and personality were adorable. He was also sleeping all through the night, and if the mother gets a good night's sleep, it goes a long way to helping her cope through the day, irrespective of whether she has a typical or atypical child.

Spring then arrived and I felt much more positive about life, especially since I was working part-time, interacting with friends and colleagues.

Chapter 7

Great News after Bad News

I menstruated about six months after having Alex, without any complications. I returned to see Mr Fisher for the tests he wanted to carry out when Alex was about ten months old. I had a hysterosalpingogram, which is an X-ray test that examines the inside of the uterus and fallopian tubes and the surrounding area. I was delighted to hear that everything seemed normal and we need not fear becoming pregnant. As if it would be possible! I had been very anxious about my reproductive organs just before the tests.

Simon wanted nature to take its course, but I had voiced how I really did not want to become pregnant yet, with Alex being so young, even if it were possible. Simon kindly remarked, 'Oh, Ali, you know that is so unlikely. If you could get pregnant you would want to shout it from the rooftops.' I think he was worried about my optimism. But I somehow felt that we may be able to conceive without medical intervention. Stranger things have happened and I had a good feeling about it.

My period was late in May, and I had a metallic taste in my mouth, which I had not experienced when expecting Alex. I told Simon I thought I may be pregnant. Again, he thought I was imagining it or being overly optimistic. He did not ridicule me, but he said, 'Oh, Ali, come off it! That is very doubtful.' I decided he was probably right and ignored it. Time flew by and soon I was two weeks overdue. I bought a pregnancy testing kit. The instructions said that if there was a pregnancy, the liquid would turn pale blue, when one or two days overdue.

THE LIQUID TURNED LIKE BLUE QUINK INK!

We were absolutely indescribably amazed, dumbfounded and happy! It was completely unbelievable. I tried not to be too ecstatic. I made an appointment with my GP to have total confirmation. After the test, the nurse came in to the waiting-room and, knowing my history, she was smiling and singing 'Congratulations!' I was immediately referred back to Mr Fisher. He said that my ease of conception was probably purely mechanical, in that carrying Alex had made my womb less retroverted and straightened my fallopian tubes. Whatever it was, to us it was an amazing miracle. I know with full certainty I can pin-point the date of conception.

Life is seldom easy and I had to listen to Mr Fisher, who looked quite serious. I remember his words verbatim, although it was about twenty-five years ago now. 'Young lady, I do not know how this pregnancy will turn out. Take each day as it comes. We still cannot be sure how strong and capable your womb is. You could lose the baby and the womb. Every night for a few months, lie down on the bed for ten minutes with your legs in the air. This may help your womb settle in a good position. Please don't count on a baby yet. If it does progress, you will have a caesarean at thirty-six weeks. There is no way I can let that womb cope with a normal delivery. It would probably split and thirty-six weeks is the deadline so the womb must not get too enlarged. I want to see you in the clinic every two weeks.'

I am not sure I properly processed this unwelcome news. All we could do was hope for the best. We tried not to be too confident about the outcome. Once again, we were totally taken aback. I did not dare be excited and tried not to think about being lucky enough to have two children. We could only live each day as it came. Fortunately, having a busy life meant there was little time to dwell on things.

Well-meaning friends said things like, 'I expect having Alex made you relaxed,' or 'Your hormones kicked in.' I know they were delighted for us and many of them asked if I was going to have an amniocentesis. Some of them made it sound like 'you are not so odd after all.' Others were unthinkingly curious and, we thought, impertinent. The private matter of whether we were going to have an amniocentesis did not feel like coffee time conversation.

Chapter 8

Ante-Natal Tests

I got to about sixteen weeks pregnant, busy working and looking after lovely Alex, who was so good-natured, sleeping well, absolutely adorable and very smiley. The Down's syndrome doesn't seem so obvious when they are babies; in many ways they seem just like all babies, who cannot walk or talk at a young age.

Mr Fisher suggested an amniocentesis, bearing in mind what the geneticist had said. Also, I did not think we could cope with two children with special needs. It is easy to say, 'Let's have the test,' though. The implications need to be well considered. One is obviously hoping the test will reveal a healthy baby has been formed, but it may not. There is no point having the test unless you have discussed the possible negative outcome and actions you wish to take. Simon and I did not discuss it in detail, but I know neither of us wanted to cope with two chromosomally impaired children. Unfortunately, having an amniocentesis is not without the risk of miscarriage. This also crossed my mind; how absolutely devastating to lose a healthy baby due to the procedure, especially with our history. I don't know if I was more anxious about the amniocentesis results or the fear of miscarriage.

The day of my amniocentesis came. My mother took Alex for the day and night, and Mr Fisher treated me with kid gloves. He told me to take a week off work, which I am sure was overkill. He also told me to rest all afternoon. He said I may lose fluid vaginally, and if so, I was to be brought straight back to hospital. With fear and trepidation, I gingerly moved about and wrapped myself in cotton wool. It was a very hot day, and I sat in the garden and fell asleep. I woke up slightly hot and sweaty. Was that fluid leaking, or was I just a bit moist? I decided I was just hot.

After a long two weeks we were given the wonderful news that our baby was chromosomally normal. Fortunately, we did not have to think about any future action with the pregnancy at that stage. This was marvellous, a step in the right direction and one less hurdle to think about, but still way to go, with carrying the baby to thirty-six weeks.

Chapter 9

Second Pregnancy

The pregnancy proceeded well and after about thirty-two weeks I was having weekly checks. Mr Fisher said he would ask me to have an elective caesarean at about thirty-six weeks, probably on a Thursday, which was my clinic day. My father's birthday was on January 25th, and I hoped Mr Fisher would not choose a date too close to that. I thought how terrible it would be if something went wrong. I would always be reminded of it on Dad's birthday, not that one would ever forget, and all Dad's future birthdays would be touched by sadness. I had this feeling that Mr Fisher would opt for January 12th, or thereabouts, which he had intimated the week before. We were all prepared, bag packed and ready to go, and Mum would have Alex. I was sent home after the clinic that day and told to be prepared for the following week. I was to be pregnant for another week, God willing. More cooking for the freezer, and lots of rest.

On Thursday January 19th, at my morning clinic appointment, Mr Fisher said, 'Right, I want you back here at two for a caesarean later, about four.' My heart was pounding, adrenalin flowing, and I was very nervously excited. I could not get hold of Simon as we did not have mobile phones then, but I told my parents. Mum took Alex and Dad drove me back to the hospital with my ready-packed bags. We called at Simon's office and luckily he was there and we told him, so he could be there for the delivery at about four.

I was taken down to theatre with Simon by my side. It was very exciting and worrying. I had managed to get this far with the pregnancy, without any of the anxieties raised by Mr Fisher arising. The delivery was smooth and without problems, as far as we knew, anyway. I wanted a girl, but would have been equally delighted with a boy, of course. I felt we were having a girl, but that was just a mother's hunch. Mr Fisher said 'it's a' —it felt as if there was a long gap—'girl!' Our darling daughter was born, 4lbs.13oz, at 4.20 pm. We were ecstatic. They took our nameless little baby to the SCBU, since she was only 4 lbs. 13 oz., but assured me she was fine. I remember being moved to my own room in a welcoming warm bed, with a cup of tea which was like sweet nectar. Simon had contacted various friends and relatives and in no time at all some beautiful flowers arrived in a pretty pink basket from our good friends, John and Zoe, with a card saying, 'Well done!' I felt so happy. I was a hundred per cent convinced that our daughter was 'typical', free from any untoward conditions. I don't like to write that I thought she was 'normal'.

Note the date, exactly one year on from returning to work after having Alex. It is strange how different life can be just one year on, with very different emotional circumstances.

I had previously asked our paediatrician, Doctor Lieberman, to check our new baby on arrival and reassure us that everything was OK, as far as anyone can tell at birth. He said he would come as soon as possible after the baby's birth, but, as it turned out, he was delayed, having gone home before he knew that our baby had arrived.

I think I have been genetically programmed to be optimistic and somehow I felt our baby was fine, so I was not concerned that he didn't come that day. I slept well and he arrived quite early the following day, bringing our new baby to me. He carried out visual and other newborn checks, and I know he would have conferred with the doctors in the SCBU.

He confirmed that our new baby daughter had passed her newborn tests. Many conditions may go undetected until later, it is true, but we were very grateful, and relieved, so far.

.

Chapter 10

Two Babies to Look After

Simon and I were over the moon to have a healthy daughter. We were so elated with all the cards, flowers, gifts and visits we had from well-wishers. This was how we should have felt after Alex's birth, but at least we had, at last, managed to produce a beautiful, healthy baby girl. We called her Charlotte Elizabeth and we adored her.

I found it hard looking after two babies with a nineteen months age gap, especially as Charlotte cried a lot. I think colic is a misnomer, but that is what she appeared to have.

Please do not think I am complaining. It was just that we had such mixed emotions, even though we had at last produced two babies, and we were exhausted, so I am not going to say how easy it was with two babies under two and one with special needs. I imagine it was like having twins; we had two babies who needed feeding by us, two babies in nappies, two babies who could not walk and who seemed to need everything simultaneously, not to mention I'd had two caesareans within nineteen months. Life was extremely busy, tiring but fun. I tried to dismiss any negative thoughts I had about the age gap between Alex and Charlotte being so close, telling myself that I should have felt extremely lucky. But however lucky we were, it was difficult raising them both, not least because of the physical toll it took.

We had been accustomed to a placid baby with Down's syndrome, and now we had to get used to a typical baby who cried incessantly, suffering wind, colic and the usual baby problems.

One particular wet Sunday, both babies were crying a lot, and I knew Simon wanted to work on his race car in the garage, but I often needed help, especially then, just so I could cook our dinner. Simon was disgruntled and he made some inappropriate comment, as I saw it, about how exasperating it was, to which I retorted, 'What did you want me to do then, have an abortion?'

Well-meaning people say one should make the most of them being young, and how quickly they grow, which I know is true, but it does not mean there are not fraught times. I do my best to help and encourage those mothers I meet who are going through the same experience. My parents and in-laws were very kind and helped out a lot. My mother often took Alex for the day or night, and left me to concentrate on the baby. I loved taking Charlotte out on her own. She had such pretty little dresses, lacy tights and hair bows and, I feel bad for saying it, it was so nice to be out with a 'typical' baby. I did not have to discuss babies with special needs and for a short while I could pretend that I did not have a special needs baby to cope with. It was a breath of fresh air.

Alex started going to a special needs nursery for two days a week, and I really appreciated this break.

At weekends I longed for Simon to be at home to help out, but unfortunately he used to get frequent migraines and be laid low in bed. I know he couldn't help it, but it was distressing, although it pales into insignificance now. I remember telling my mother I could not cope with a disabled son and a disabled husband, but that is what it often felt like.

I had lots of help, though, and I realise how fortunate I was. Our health visitor knew the tutor at a local college which ran a Nursery

Nurse and Childcare course, so I was sent students who needed work experience to help me out. This was so nice, just to have someone make a cup of tea when I didn't have time, or change a nappy, but of course the students could do far more than this, and I think they in turn gained some valuable experience. It was so nice to have a young person around and I could have a bath in peace.

I am not going to dwell much on the early years and coping with two children, because we always realised what a miracle Charlotte was. She walked before Alex, at the age of one, and Alex walked soon after her. As she grew up and progressed, Alex had a role model to look up to and copy. This was not always good, of course, but mostly it was. They both used to run off in the street and, I am ashamed to say, I found it very hard taking them both out on my own, since they would run off, in opposite directions, and they fiercely opposed wearing reins, so it became an arduous undertaking, or they would try to climb out of the pushchair. I think I was a nice mother, but not necessarily a good one, with respect to discipline. I often came home in tears, having found it very hard controlling them both in the street. Down's syndrome children do tend to wander off, and I assume Charlotte copied Alex. A man we know with fourteen children saw me in the street once and remarked, 'Goodness, you have your hands full!'

One day, Alex and I were watching a lorry out of the window. I thought he would enjoy it. I had a nice bowl of three plants on the window ledge. Alex was in a good mood, so I know it was not out of malice. Perhaps he thought the bowl was in the way, but, for whatever reason, he picked it up and threw it down. What a mess! Soil and plants everywhere. I was so upset; we had been having a nice time and it had backfired. Luckily, my mother was there. I cried and said, 'I don't want him,' which was overly dramatic, but I felt sure the accident had happened because of his lack of awareness and small brain. My mother, sweet and supportive as usual, said, 'I know it is hard for you sometimes.' We cleared up and carried on, as you do.

Although children grow up quickly, and all parents wonder where the years have gone, I am so glad those early years have passed, since it was quite stressful, even though we were so lucky to have had two children, and I know there are and always will be many people who would give anything to have a child.

I remember one time when the phone was ringing, the potatoes were boiling over, one of them was being sick and the other had the top off the Ribena, and I needed the bathroom. I did not know what to see to first, but that is normal family life with young children.

The main issue was safety. Naturally, I did not want them to come to any harm running in the street or reaching for hot drinks, and Alex had no sense of danger until much older than typical children.

I remember strapping them both in their car seats before a birthday party. The car was parked at the front door and I had left the door open so I could hear what was going on. While I rushed back in to put some make-up on, I heard a loud scream. I tore outside to see Alex holding a tuft of Charlotte's hair which he had pulled out. I felt so neglectful. I remember wishing that there was a slightly bigger age gap between them, because they were such a handful, however delightful a handful, but that was something over which we'd had no control.

One Christmas, while cooking dinner, Simon actually locked me in the kitchen for safety reasons, so I could remove the hot turkey from the oven without two toddlers pulling at my clothes trying to 'help' me and see what I was doing. They were both so busy all the time and wanting to be right by me, which was lovely, if not difficult sometimes.

One day, when Alex was two, he was playing in his sandpit quite happily. I saw this wasp approach, and yes, you guessed it, I couldn't prevent Alex being stung, right by his eye. I was worried since the area swelled very quickly, increasingly large. I bathed it with vinegar and shot Alex to the Accident and Emergency Department of our hospital, probably overreacting, but it was a nasty swelling and so near his eye, and my father was away so I couldn't confer with him.

A doctor treated Alex nicely and then looked at me and said, 'Is he subnormal?' I was completely taken aback. I felt like saying, 'So? You are ugly.' It was so unnecessary and hurtful.

A much lovelier occasion was the Bourn Hall 'Celebrate IVF Babies' party. One lovely summer day, we all four set off for this party, Alex and Charlotte smartly dressed, double buggy at the ready. We strolled round the beautiful grounds, enjoying the company of friends we had made from Bourn Hall. The children loved it because there was plenty to do, with age-appropriate rides for all the babies and children. There were hundreds and hundreds of babies and children conceived by IVF, and it was so amazing to be part of it. A large group photo was taken, which we will always treasure. It was exciting and rewarding for the staff, too, to see the results of their hard work and commitment. This was evident by their faces of sheer joy!

The pioneering work by Mr Patrick Steptoe and Robert Edwards, and many others, for IVF is so incredible that I find it impossible to properly express our gratitude.

I did think of those less fortunate, though.

Alex and Charlotte, two years and seven months respectively

Chapter 11

Choosing a First School

Alex attended a special needs nursery and a playgroup for 'typical' children. The staff at both were really sweet, helpful and kind. Our lovely Portage helper, Helen, advised me about schools, and even came with me to visit them, which was invaluable, bearing in mind she had her own son with Down's syndrome, six years older than Alex. There was one mother who, I felt, looked at Alex as though he should not be attending the playgroup for typical children, which was very upsetting. When Alex was at playgroup, this mother stared and ushered her child away as if he were an alien. I thought she was frumpy, fat and looked old and I didn't want her near Alex either. It may be childish, but this thought-retaliation helps you cope with such people.

We could have let Alex attend the special needs nursery full time, and then he would probably progress to the affiliated special needs primary section. We knew he would have been extremely well cared for, but it was a severe learning difficulty (SLD) school. This meant he could have been too cosseted, and we were advised to seek a mainstream education, for as many years as seemed appropriate. In the country of the blind, the one-eyed man is king, and indeed, Alex seemed like a king at the SLD nursery, in that he could walk, run and talk a little. It would have made life very easy if Alex were to attend the SLD nursery, as he would be collected from home and delivered back, and there would be no demands on him like homework and playground roughness. But that might not be fair on him. He needed maximum stimulation and input, so we chose a mainstream nursery, where, happily, the headmaster and staff welcomed him with open arms. I also feared the reactions of other parents, but I need not have done. All the staff and parents were absolutely wonderful in their approach and acceptance, especially after the playgroup experience.

The less grown-up children are, the less the differential shows between a Down's syndrome child and a typical one. Not many three-year-olds read, so comparisons are limited and the differences in abilities are not flung in your face so easily.

In the very first few weeks of being at nursery, Alex was invited to a twins' birthday party, which I was extremely happy about. I introduced myself to their mother and I still see her occasionally now. I did feel the need to send him to the party in a nappy, in case of accidents, which embarrassed me, since I did not know the mother very well. She, of course, was charming about it, but this is another extra problem with a young Down's syndrome child, since he was already aged four.

The school hired an extremely warm and friendly lady called Ingrid, who worked with Alex one to one for all his nursery, primary and junior school days. Ingrid was an absolute godsend, who grew to become extremely fond of Alex and this was definitely reciprocated. She was there daily to help Alex. I knew we could count on her to look after Alex, watch over him and help him to read, use scissors and all the other things the children were learning. Ingrid would report back on anything we needed to know and put our minds at rest regarding his progress or other matters.

Alex was regularly invited to the other children's parties and outings, and was accepted as an equal by the children. In short, he had many friends and he was enjoying school.

One day, a new boy arrived at the school from America and he and Alex played together. The mother kindly asked Alex to tea. Soon after, she said, 'We had never heard of Down's syndrome and we rushed to find out about it and look it up.' I suppose this was quite sensible, but nevertheless, it sounded a little outspoken and slightly hurtful. Having lived and breathed Down's syndrome for about six years, I was slightly stunned, but I know she did not mean to upset me; she was just being frank.

One parents' evening at school, when Alex was about six, I felt the meeting was going well. The teacher said that Alex could do this and that, and how he had friends and various other positive things. We discussed how pleasantly amazed we were when we realised that Alex could spell 'giraffe'. Then, out of the blue, the teacher asked what we were going to do when Alex was an adult. I was dumbfounded. It wasn't that we had buried our heads in the sand regarding the future, but I didn't know what we were having for dinner that night, so I definitely was not thinking about fourteen years' time. [I felt it was so unnecessary and hurtful, both impertinent and irrelevant. Was she going to ask the other parents of six-year- olds what profession or job their children might be interested in later life?]

When Alex was about seven, the headmaster dropped a bombshell: he wanted Alex to stay down a year. We held several meetings and phone calls. To us, this was a massive mistake. Alex had friends in his peer group. Also, he would never catch up with this group, however many years he stayed down and, we felt that having friends he knew, who had already accepted him, was his biggest asset at school. We could have fought this tooth and nail, but we needed the school's support, so extremely reluctantly, we agreed. It was heart-breaking in the beginning of the new school year. I asked Alex how he was getting on, if he liked the new classmates. He looked sad and said, 'What are their names?' Of course, he still had Ingrid, but it was obvious that it was going to take him a long time to settle in and for the children to get to know and accept him. Waiting for him to come out after school one day, all the children came running out in groups, and Alex strolled along the playground alone. I felt so sad.

Overall things turned out all right, and Alex did get some party and tea invitations, but we cannot help wondering if it would have been better for Alex to have remained in the original class. Simon and I both felt that Alex never achieved the same friendships with this new class as he had with his previous one. One day the teacher summoned me to say Alex had hit another boy, Philip. Naturally, I was embarrassed and surprised. The teacher was very nice about it and, I suppose to minimize my anxiety, she said not to worry about it. 'Between you and me,' she said, she wished she could hit Philip sometimes, too, because he was a really annoying child. Not politically correct, perhaps, but it was obvious she was trying to make light of it for my sake.

All the time we wondered if mainstream school was the best option. I think it was, since Alex could watch and observe and learn, as far as he was able. He learnt to read, write and swim and to use a computer. Of course, his reading and writing ability is still fairly limited, but he can read a menu, an easy book, write thank you letters, compose and send emails and use a mobile phone, sending text messages, saving contacts' details and, rather too frequently, phoning.

We always worried if any of the other children would bully him, tease him or be unkind to him. Overall, I would say this did not occur. Happily, too, there was Ingrid to keep an eye on him.

Every parent wants their child to reach their potential and do well. The more able we wanted Alex to be, the more he would realise he was different. I am not sure how much he was aware that he was less able. It is not an easy subject to discuss with your Down's syndrome child. Alex never asked at this stage why he could not do this, that and the other. All the other children were taken to and from school, so Alex was not unusual in that respect and he didn't need to ask why he couldn't walk alone to school, or indeed go anywhere alone.

Alex took part in the Christmas plays, sports days and general school activities, and in general we like to think he thrived, under the circumstances. He went on school trips such as 'PGL' holidays (named after Peter Gordon Lawrence). These are action-packed outward bound activities for school children and Alex took part in all activities like abseiling and canoeing. He could do his own packing and was really excited to go away without Mum and Dad, for five days at a time. These were massive milestones, and it was extremely rewarding that he could accomplish so much. With typical children, you can easily take it for granted that they will manage some of these activities. Feedback from him and the staff was always good.

Alex and Charlotte, three years and eighteen months respectively

Alex's first day at school, September 1992

Alex at sports day.

Chapter 12

Secondary School

Time passed quickly, and soon we had to consider secondary schools. The mainstream schools were enormous, with large classes. It was obvious Alex would never come close to keeping up, even with support. Would it be fair on him, the school, the other pupils and the staff to keep him in mainstream? Also, I did not think I could drop him at mainstream secondary school and go off to work without extreme angst. I imagined all sorts of bullying and other problems. I am not sure Ingrid would have wanted to carry on with her support, or indeed if we would have received funding for her. Alex was toilet trained but if he was slightly unwell, he may not get to the toilet in time, which was just one worry.

It's amazing how problems are viewed between typical children and those with special needs. For instance, when Charlotte was about seven, her school phoned one day to say she was not well; she had been sick. I went to fetch her and I did not feel awkward that she was unwell. Why would I? When it was Alex who had a gastrointestinal upset at school, I was very embarrassed. It may sound silly, but that's how it is. You do not want anyone thinking, 'Oh, it's because he has Down's syndrome, he didn't get to the toilet in time,' or, 'Poor mother, having to deal with that.'

I would say that Alex did not have behavioural problems, or at least, if he did, they were few and far between, and no different from most typical children. He did push a little friend of his down a few stairs one day. Fortunately, the little girl was not harmed, but I was extremely embarrassed and upset. One of the other mothers kindly took me aside to comfort me. I was crying and exclaiming, 'I don't want him,' but this was very short-lived and Alex apologised. If a typical child had done it, there would have been less upset and I would probably not have over-reacted to such an extent.

So, after careful consideration, meetings at schools, visits to mainstream schools and a moderate learning difficulty school (MLD school) in our borough, we opted for an MLD school. This school had very good facilities, understanding and capable staff and transport was provided to and from school. Having made this choice, we remember feeling that a considerable weight had been lifted off our shoulders.

An MLD school gave us great peace of mind compared with a mainstream school, especially at the senior school level due to class sizes and adolescent differences.

On his first day at senior school, we were waiting for a car or minibus which was coming to collect him. A car pulled up outside. Naturally, I didn't want to put him in any car without checking it was the correct one, so I asked the driver, 'Who have you come for?', to which he replied, 'Dunno, love, I just got the address.' I then asked the driver his name, so I could say to Alex, 'This is John' or whoever. The driver said, 'Who wants to know?' Can you believe it? Suffice it to say, I worried until I had established that Alex got to school safe and sound. The drivers were all nice but they took a bit of getting used to.

The school was always positive about Alex. He had a cheery nature, a sense of humour, made some friends and, relative to many of the other children, who had a wide range of disabilities, Alex continued to learn and did well, considering the Down's syndrome.

Meeting with his friends out of school was not so easy since the MLD school catered for children within a fourteen mile radius, so the children were more scattered than Alex's primary school friends, not to mention negotiating the school transport system if he wanted to invite friends to tea or accept invitations after school. Despite these difficulties, Alex did have three particular good friends with whom he could socialise regularly.

The staff were all so helpful, reassuring and really pleasant. Parents' evening was a joy, listening to the encouraging words about Alex and his capabilities. Of course, we listened with rose-coloured glasses, not knowing whether Alex would be able to live independently, drive a car or do many of the tasks which typical adults can do. Some Down's syndrome people do live independently and drive, but Alex is not yet able to do so, even if he will in the future. Due to his vulnerability, we doubt it. Some Down's syndrome parents may read this and be indignant because their child does live independently and drive, but we are always thinking of his safety, wanting to strike the right balance between independence and safety.

Alex was very amenable, too. Once, at a hearing test, the audiologist said some words quietly with a book covering her mouth, to see if Alex could hear them without any lip-reading. She explained to him that she would say 'car', and other everyday words, and Alex was to repeat the word. She said, slightly condescendingly, 'Do you think you can do that, Alex?' To which he replied, 'I will spell them if you like.'

Alex went on school trips, as he did in junior school, for five days at a time. Reports from him and the staff were always good, as before. There were no real upsets and overall his time at secondary school went very smoothly. Alex passed various exams, including French, Drama, Design and Technology, at Entry Level 2, in 2004.

In 2006, he was awarded second grade modules from the National Skills profile in number skills, which include understanding time and using numbers and money. He also had an Award Scheme Development and Accreditation Network (ASDAN) award for 'Towards Independence', which includes Meal Preparation, Horticulture, using a computer and Out in The Community. His art work was very interesting, and the art teacher, whom Alex hero-worshipped, suggested that he may be able to do art GCSE. Unfortunately, the school changed their mind about this, but we were thrilled that it had been considered. After cookery lessons, he often brought the cooked items home, including cakes and lasagne.

Alex did say to Simon and me one day, 'Charlotte's more clever than me, isn't she?' Simon said, 'She is 'cleverer' than me, too,' which we hope reassured him.

When Alex was about fifteen the school started to discuss 'the future', the dreaded future for children like Alex. It was a bed of roses whilst at secondary school, even if we didn't think so at the time, since transport was arranged and Alex was occupied and happy. The first decision was to say that Alex would like to stay at school for the sixth form. Apart from this being the best situation for him, to enhance any learning, it meant that we were able to think things through about his future. We were not burying our heads in the sand, but it gave us more time for research and enquiries. The school's Head of Sixth Form and the Connexions advisor were extremely helpful, supportive and knowledgeable about the options.

Connexions is a service provided by the government for a wide range of young people who need help with their careers. Once again, we were extremely lucky. The school decided to do a Year 14 for Alex and two of his friends, with a specially devised programme of cooking, road safety, numeracy and various other life skills. The woman in charge of them said she had total confidence in Alex's road safety and capability of crossing roads at this stage.

Because he had stayed down in junior school, and with the Year 14 at secondary school, it meant he was twenty when he left school in July 2007. My father always said, 'It's an ill wind that does not blow some good,' and so I believed that although we were bitterly disappointed when Alex stayed down in primary school, it meant we had gained another year with him at home and at school, which, ultimately, was to everyone's advantage.

In 2005/06 we had started to pursue the options for Alex's next steps. These included local colleges and residential colleges for special needs young adults. Simon and I wanted Alex to go to a residential college for his sake. We felt this would give him maximum help towards independence, the opportunity for him to socialise with peers as opposed to being with his old parents, and it would be more fun and rewarding. Apart from anything else, Charlotte was going off to university at the same time and we thought Alex would feel 'grown up' by also going away to college.

This decision was not taken lightly. We are not going to live forever and we needed to be reassured that Alex could manage without us after our demise. This is one of the scariest things to consider: what happens after we are gone?

A friend had told me about a Down's syndrome young man living with his widowed mother in her street. The widowed mother died unexpectedly, and my friend never saw the young man again. She had no idea what happened to him. Whether he was taken into care or sent to a relative, no one knew. We were determined that nothing like this would happen to Alex.

It sounds easy to say we wanted Alex to attend a residential college. The biggest hurdle was obtaining funding. There were many seemingly appropriate colleges. In fact, the Connexions adviser handed us a thick book detailing these colleges and their curriculum. Every year funding cuts impeded pupils' acceptance, and we were warned that we were extremely unlikely to get funding for Alex. You have to prove a local non-residential college cannot offer you the same facilities. Although local colleges cannot offer the same out-of-daytime-hours, social interactions, independent living help and so on, still we were warned of the possibility of being unsuccessful in our quest.

There were quite a few residential colleges which looked suitable, but none was very near to us. The problem is, these colleges are very expensive, owing to the facilities, level of care and support staff required. We were told that parents are not allowed to contribute, even if they can afford it, as that would probably slowly but surely end the otherwise free to parents, local authority-funded places for other students.

The message is clear: push back at all obstacles and fight with all your might to obtain funding, if that is what you want. I cannot tell you how many meetings, letters and college visits were necessary. We applied to a college in Redhill in 2006 for entry in 2007 and Alex was interviewed in the spring of 2006. We were very excited. It seemed perfect, not too far away from home, and Alex knew two students who were already there. Whilst our application was being considered we received a letter informing us, totally unexpectedly, that this college would be closing down and we should pursue other options. One step forwards and two back. Needless to say, we were very downhearted. Our Connexions adviser suggested we look at Queen Alexandra College (QAC) in Harborne, Birmingham. Once again, we were filling in application forms and visiting colleges. We were very impressed with QAC and the staff and, in early 2007, we had a very favourable outcome. QAC wrote to say Alex had a place starting in September 2007, subject to funding, and our Connexions adviser telephoned me at work soon after to say Alex had been granted funding. Naturally, we were extremely relieved. Alex had had an assessment at the college involving a twenty-four-hour stay, which he had thoroughly enjoyed, and the staff had said they thought he would fit in very well.

Most parents feel sad when their child leaves school, thinking of their next chapter in life, what is to come, and this was no exception. The special needs aspect and leaving caring staff behind made it harder to move on. I was away on business when Alex left secondary school, so I missed his 'prom night', but we felt very proud of his leaving photos and school reports.

Alex and Charlotte as teenagers

Chapter 13

Residential College

September 2007. Alex was off to Birmingham, and Charlotte to Manchester. Everybody wondered how Simon and I would cope, with both our loving children leaving the nest simultaneously.

Naturally, we spoke about it to Alex a lot, and how Charlotte was leaving, too. Charlotte would tell us how excited she was, and obviously about any worries she had. Alex seemed to be excited; I am sure he had more worries than Charlotte, but he did not really voice them. It was difficult to know what exactly he was thinking, and of course we did not want to ask him many questions in case we inadvertently put extra ideas or worries into his head.

It was a very busy time with all the preparations, things to buy and so on. Simon and I were a bit daunted but also looking forward to a little more freedom. This may sound selfish, but after twenty years of our devoted care, it seemed appropriate for Alex to gain some independence in the next stage of his life and we knew he would be very well cared for. The day came to take him. I felt slightly sick and worried. I kept reassuring him all would be well; if he wasn't happy he need not stay. We reminded him about the fun he had had at his overnight assessment. But I just didn't know what was going through his mind, and if he was scared.

The college chose Saturdays for all new starters in order to give them settling-in time. When we arrived and parked the car, Alex said disconcertingly, 'Oh, we are here.' Simon and I felt absolutely dreadful. How could we leave our darling son? I felt numb and tearful. The hostel staff cleverly staggered the arrival times of the four new students, so each family had their own dedicated arrival slot, thus giving us undivided attention. We helped Alex unpack, had a cup of tea and went through any paperwork. We met a few staff, who were all young and welcoming. As we hugged Alex and left, I had to keep my sunglasses on to hide the tears. I was devastated. Were we doing the right thing? How would he be? I reiterated to myself how the pain of having a disabled child was indescribable and how I wished I could keep him with me forever. No parent should have to go through this.

Simon, Charlotte and I left our gorgeous Alex in Birmingham. We were all quiet on the way home. Simon was going off with his friends for a regular annual boys' event, the date being out of his control. The timing was unfortunate. Charlotte was going out with friends. I did not mind, because I am a coper and I was quite happy to be alone with my thoughts. I cannot remember if I decided in earnest to write this book then, or much earlier, but I realised I must try and support other parents going through the same pain, if I can.

Life carried on being very busy. We had to get Charlotte ready for her first term at university. Leaving her at Manchester was far less stressful than leaving Alex. As we left Charlotte on her first day in the hall of residence, I had a lump in my throat, but we drove away leaving her chatting and giggling to some girls she had just met.

Alex did not use a mobile phone in those days, so we could not speak for a while. I managed to get some sleep that first night he was away, and the hostel manager very kindly phoned me on the Sunday morning to say all was well. After we had left, Alex had met the other new students. There were about eight students in his hostel, of whom four were new. They had played some games outside, had supper and played music, predominantly Elvis Presley music, Alex's favourite. RELIEF! It seemed Alex was absolutely fine and we spoke that evening. He settled in very well and we spoke about twice a week, plus he knew he could contact me anytime if he had any worries by asking the hostel staff to phone me. After six weeks it was half term and he came home for ten days.

Alex made two particular friends, a blind girl called Genna, and Rebecca. They all started together. Alex was also very fond of his key worker, Chris, and another member of staff called Paul. After Chris left during Alex's first year, Paul became Alex's favourite member of staff from the hostel. They have an extremely good relationship and share many interests, including heavy metal music and computer games and they both have a good sense of humour. Paul is extremely caring and it is obvious how fond they are of each other. I know Alex was very happy. He is still in touch with Rebecca.

We asked Alex if he locked the bathroom door whilst in the hostel. 'Oh, yes,' he said, 'or Genna might come in.' This answer surprised us because poor Genna was blind—or did he not fully understand the meaning of blind?

The college was really good, the staff being very caring and fun, and with the hostel being in the college grounds, we were extremely happy with the set up. Some students progress from this hostel to one slightly further away after a year, but it was decided to keep Alex in the same hostel, as it was felt that he needed the maximum help and close proximity to the college. This was fine with us, since we could see he was better off staying put; he wanted the comfort zone of the same bedroom, same staff and general continuity.

When Alex got accepted to the College, we were told that funding was for a minimum of two years, and, if it could be seen that he was making progress, a third year's funding would automatically follow. We discovered that this was not necessarily the case. When Alex returned for his second year and I enquired about securing a third year of funding, I was told that one person left at the end of the second year without knowing if they were coming back for a third. How terrible is that? Imagine telling your special needs young adult, or any student, 'Sorry, not sure what is going to happen after the summer holidays.' This was not the fault of the college, but the borough where the person lived. I know that the pot of money is not bottomless, but it seems so hard on these under-privileged people with their special needs. I can only write about the parents' feelings here, and not the allocation of precious funds awarded to local authorities. It is a great shame to have to fight for funding for young adults with special needs when vast sums are spent on various extravagant-seeming projects.

I was determined, if possible, that Alex and we would not have to go through this, not knowing early on in year two if a third year could be funded. So we started making applications for a third year of funding. This was yet another enormous task involving numerous emails, phone calls and meetings with the college staff, our local borough education staff and Connexions adviser, and our MP. We did have to visit a local day college and speak with the head tutor, who said that her college could not offer anything like Alex was receiving at Birmingham and that their course was a backward step from what he had already done. This information was vital to our application. All this was so time-consuming. It seemed so unfair that the third year existed with a specially designed programme, but that Alex might not be able to partake of it.

Towards the end of year two, we still had not heard if Alex had funding for his third year. It was difficult to pursue other options, since we hoped more than anything that he would be successful.

We felt the third year would underpin and reinforce his learning. After all, the college had a third year course planned to enhance years one and two, and we had not prepared Alex for the possibility of his time being cut short.

The swine flu outbreak had started, and term was due to end, and still we had no news of his further education. The college had to close unexpectedly early, owing to the swine flu. They phoned and said please come and fetch all students. This was about three days before the end of term. On this same day, we had a call from our local authority to say Alex had a third year of funding! We were overjoyed. We fully realised how lucky we had been, too. I know life is full of ups and downs for everybody, but I believe rarely more so than when you have special needs offspring.

We enjoyed our summer holiday, realising soon after the next college year started in September 2009, that the fun would begin again. What next in July 2010, when Alex left college for good?

Where the children are concerned, change takes me a while to process. It was very hard leaving Alex each time at college, even though he was clean, warm, safe and happy. It was also hard bringing him home, worrying about him being looked after whilst we were at work and arranging things for him to do. He is fine at home alone for short periods, but that does not mean that we do not worry about it.

On Alex's last day at college, with us all feeling very daunted about the future, including Alex as well, since he had made many friends and had been very happy there, the staff said they were setting up a supported living programme and asked if we would be interested. Simon and I both instantly felt a huge weight off our minds. We did not need to discuss it; we both knew exactly how we felt, just by looking at each other. We knew it would take time and effort for the staff to set up, but we were sure it was the right way forward for Alex. We approached him gingerly about it in the car coming home. Very casually, we discussed with Alex how Simon and I do not live with our parents any more, and how his cousins had moved out from home and lived without their parents, and did he think he might like to live in Birmingham with some of his college friends, and have Paul as a key worker? We waited for his reply with trepidation, before Alex exclaimed, 'I can't wait for it to happen!'

This was such a wonderful positive outcome, especially since Paul and Alex had a great relationship. One of the college staff, Alan, was setting up this new 'Independence Plus' project. Alex also knew Alan well, and was very fond of him, too. Alan produced an annual show with the students, and Alex often had a musical part in these shows.

We knew he was sad about leaving the college. He had been given some adorable photos, cards and presents, not to mention a full size Elvis suit. He hugged the staff and his friends. We drove home feeling much happier about the future, even if it was going to take some time and planning.

Our personal feeling is that whilst we hope and know that Charlotte will watch out for Alex, and visit him regularly, we realise that he is not her responsibility, and we would not expect her to look after him. She is his sister, not one of his parents. I know she will always love and be caring to him, but she should not be under any obligation. We feel quite strongly about this, because I have met some families where the mother has said to me that she expects her child/children to care for the disabled sibling, and whilst they might volunteer to do so, it should be of their own accord and not expected by the parents. I am sure different cultures have different customs, though.

Chapter 14

Life after Residential College

It is fair to say that Simon and I pulled the wool over our eyes with certain aspects of Alex's life and his possible progression. Whilst residential college was absolutely great for him, and we certainly appreciated how lucky we were to secure the three-year place, it still meant we could not forget our son had a learning disability.

Alex learnt many things at college. With support, he could now do his laundry, go shopping for food, help prepare and cook it, clear up the kitchen, change his bed and more. His reading, writing, numeracy, computer skills and the general health and safety aspects of everyday life were more firmly embedded. He passed various exams, including Asdan Towards Independence Using a Computer, Citizenship and Money. He also received a City and Guilds certificate for Personal Progression through Practical Life, which includes using community facilities, practical project work, developing creative skills and keeping fit and healthy. He also received a pass at Entry level for oral communication skills from the English Speaking Board and an eDigital Competence Certificate for word processing.

These are all achievements which reflect Alex's competencies. Along with Alex, we can be proud that he has mastered these skills, but nothing can take away that wretched extra chromosome from every cell of his body. Not that we expected it to. Alex had had a great advantage, but he was still a twenty-four-year-old with Down's syndrome and the worries cannot and do not go away. He still needs a sheltered environment with a modified life.

Someone said to us that if Alex can use a computer, he should be able to get a job easily, but people don't realise how that extra chromosome affects the individual, their abilities, however good, and their vulnerability.

I remember being very worried about Alex leaving and us all adjusting to him living at home again. Charlotte was also leaving university and hoping to find a job. It was a very difficult time for new graduates to find work, as it still is today. Nevertheless, we were confident Charlotte would get some sort of job eventually, even if temporary and not something of her final choice, or an unpaid internship for experience. The college suggested Alex might be able to get a voluntary job, which hopefully could materialise into something permanent. We knew he would need support with any job. He said he might want to work at a supermarket, collecting the trolleys in the car park. I did think this would be a slight worry with the possibility of pushing the trolleys into cars or people. Without being negative, these thoughts are inevitably at the back of your mind. I did not want to be told by one of the customers, 'My Porsche has a huge scratch on it, from the supermarket trolley in the car park.'

Soon after Alex and Charlotte came back to live at home, we went on a family summer holiday. Soon after, my darling father, aged ninety-one and very frail, passed away. Life was certainly turned totally upside down: both children home and jobless, the loss of the father I adored, watching over my mother, and then my mother-in-law broke her hip and hospitalised. No time to wallow. This is all part and parcel of family life for people in their middle years, but things seem to come in clusters.

We had been enquiring about a day centre for Alex to attend, which had a place for him three days a week. To me, 'day centre' conjured up a place where people congregated and vegetated. Not so for Alex. His day centre should be considered an extremely well catered-for centre for mixed ability adults with wide ranging opportunities and with excellent staff. It is called CMSS in Northwood Hills. When it first opened, CMSS stood for Central Middlesex Spastic Society. Times have changed and that wording is no longer considered acceptable, hence it is simply called CMSS. The staff provide transport and take the clients on day trips, residential holiday and shopping outings. They provide a vast range of activities to suit all abilities, from cooking, acting, computer skills, music and much more. Alex is very sociable and he settled in straight away, forming many friendships with staff and clients of all ages. In fact, he knew some of the CMSS clients from his school days, so it was really good for them to meet up again. During his two years living at home, Alex was happy, but he frequently asked us about going to live in Birmingham and when the supported living house would be ready and the program up and running.

Of course, much had to be accomplished by the Birmingham staff for the supported living, and Alan cannot be praised enough for working tirelessly for this to come to fruition. Nothing comes free, so money, costs and funding were the biggest challenge.

Charlotte secured a temporary job and then a permanent one, so that was one less thing to worry about.

Alex eventually moved into supported living in July 2012, two years after leaving college. He had seemed desperate to go, and since it was not absolutely certain that he could go, it was a relief in some ways when we got the go-ahead. Having said that, we had such mixed emotions about his leaving us. Selfishly, we would be more free, but to face up to the fact that if everything worked out well, our darling 'little' boy, then aged twenty-five, would be moving out was very thought-provoking. We knew Alex would come home often, and we would visit him, but it is harder to let go of a child, or young adult, with special needs rather than a 'typical' one, and that can be hard enough. We gave him a surprise leaving party, with many friends and relatives coming.

We felt both sad and happy taking him. He smiled and waved to us as we left. We just felt empty. It was a dark, rainy afternoon, and we travelled home quietly, alone with our thoughts. It was nowhere near as sad or as bad as leaving him on his first day at residential college, though.

Alex had his own mobile phone now, so we knew he could contact us easily and vice versa, which was very reassuring. His first bill was not so reassuring, since he slightly overused his phone, a big understatement, and we had obviously not chosen the best contract for his use.

We soon upgraded his phone contract.

To our delight, Alex settled well. I think we knew this was almost a given, since he knew and adored some of the staff, and also the other young adults in his house. One year has passed and Alex is enjoying himself. It takes time to set up a structured routine for five boys with differing needs, abilities and desires. For instance, one boy might love football or drama and the others not. The staff work hard to keep the boys happy, occupied and safe. Alex does swimming, bowling, car valeting, and some café work in the college and has just started working in a charity shop for two part-days a week. He has passed a food hygiene exam, at what is called Entry level, which means that he has learnt and retained some basic food hygiene knowledge and answered related questions correctly. He also plays badminton and frequently goes to the gym.

Naturally, we want him to reach his potential with respect to independence and a job, but his vulnerability has to be considered, and we are not sure what his potential is. We do not want to hold him back, but at the same time we do not want him to be unsafe, or to do anything he is not comfortable with. He told us that he would not want to go on the tube alone, so we respected his wishes. If a typical child said that, one might think how the child should be encouraged to do so since it would be in his interests, but when a child with special needs feels this way, it is a very different situation.

I recently stopped working, mainly to write this book and help my mother more. I could have retired sooner, but I didn't want to become tied to being at home every day by 3.30pm to receive Alex after CMSS. Fortunately, I had a very good, reliable carer to receive him after school and, later on, after the day centre. The biggest stress for any working mother is the childcare arrangements or, at least, re-organising them, especially when they are disrupted, and, of course, for Alex, 'childcare' arrangements were much more prolonged than for a typical child. There always had to be someone at home to receive Alex after he returned from CMSS. Perhaps it was still hard for me to accept that 'childcare' was still necessary for Alex, in his twenties, after all these years.

Alex is our son and our responsibility, but I did not want to swap working for being tied to a timetable after all the years of pursuing a career which meant having my own identity away from the Down's and maintaining my own persona with intellectual and social pursuits at work which were extremely important to me. It enabled me to have a life away from the Down's syndrome and consequently gave the family a better balance.

Alex at Summer Camp

Chapter 15

Siblings

I always feel sad when I see families with just one child, where the child has Down's syndrome. Not my business, it is true, but I cannot help wondering if they chose to have just one or if they were unable to have more. If the latter, so be it, enough said, and I hope I have not offended anyone. If it is the former, I just think they have missed out so much. It may be that they were so shell-shocked by having a Down's syndrome baby that they could not contemplate having more. It may be that they thought they wanted to concentrate on one special baby, and give the child their all. It may be they worried about having another child with needs.

Whatever the reason, I would urge parents not to give up and to have more children – after genetic counselling and subject to advice – if that is their wish. I cannot over-emphasize how the future seemed so much brighter for us once we had Charlotte. Apart from wanting a child without special needs, the sibling(s) can be company for the less fortunate child, and hopefully aid their progress. As parents, it is usually such a pleasure to raise a child, with or without developmental problems, but typical children usually have blotting paper minds, an eager-to-learn approach, and it is a joy watching them grow and progress. They generally appear to learn basic skills easily and it is a welcome relief after sometimes struggling to teach or show a child with special needs these skills, with all the extra effort and patience needed for children like Alex. Naturally, it is really rewarding when children with special needs master a new skill, but it can be stressful until they do. I know Alex has taught Charlotte a great deal about life and people, too.

We would have liked more children after Charlotte, but it was not to be. So Charlotte really is our miracle, since I don't believe I have been fertile since she was born or there would definitely have been more babies in our house.

Where the Down's syndrome baby is the first to arrive, as with us, it is massively different to having a family of healthy 'typical' children, maybe pondering another baby or wanting another one, or indeed having an accidental conception and the resulting baby having Down's syndrome. Indeed, I think our situation hardly compares. Yes, we were immeasurably devastated, but we were desperate for a baby. For a readymade 'normal' family to receive a Down's syndrome baby must be very shocking in a different way. I have met a few such families and, although everybody has different circumstances, the mothers in each case appeared to feel as if the Down's syndrome baby was a usurper in their otherwise happy unit. They had established a normal family life—if there is such a thing—and suddenly they had to accommodate this new and different baby. One such family I know attempted to have the baby adopted, but soon returned for their baby. Another such family's fourth baby unfortunately had Down's syndrome. All the siblings adored the baby and helped thereafter. Every situation is different.

Without doubt, the birth of a Down's syndrome baby creates a really sad beginning, and fear of the unknown future does not help. For siblings of Down's syndrome children there are usually difficulties. We always worried that Charlotte may get bullied at school about Alex, but this could not be further from the truth. Most of Charlotte's friends and their parents liked Alex, and were kind to him. We did decide to send Charlotte to a different school from Alex, though, because we wanted her to be 'Charlotte Lane' and not 'Alex's sister'. We didn't want her to have any problems related to Alex whilst at school.

Nevertheless, she did have problems with some people out of school because of Alex. I do know that he has caused her some embarrassment over the years. After all, it is all very well for the parents to love their Down's syndrome child, and to grow to accept him/her, but you cannot necessarily expect siblings automatically to do so. Charlotte told us that it was hard when we went on family holidays and they met other children in the swimming pool and so on. Often other children would ask, 'Is that your brother?' and stare or point at him. One woman asked Charlotte, 'What is your coping strategy with a brother like Alex?' I don't think she understood the question at age six!

When Charlotte was a teenager, typically getting embarrassed about the slightest thing, like the colour of Grandma's cardigan or my jeans, she started to bring home new boy and girl friends. She had the usual teenage excitement at the prospect of having a boyfriend and I found that she would hide pictures of Alex, since she was extremely self-conscious about the Down's. She would ask me to keep Alex in the kitchen, whereas he wanted to meet her new friends. These friends, most still friendly to this day, did eventually meet Alex and were lovely to him, and Alex loves to see them, too, but Charlotte was mortified about them meeting Alex. I totally understood, but I did want Alex to meet them. I think I was able to introduce him in a calm and sensitive way to minimise Charlotte's fears. All the friends were sweet, asking Alex about his music tastes and talking happily with him and, needless to say, they were not at all embarrassed, but Charlotte's anxiety was a normal teenage reaction and we did not want to impose any difficulties on her.

I would say that not a day goes by when I am out with Alex without someone looking at us. This is not as bad as it sounds. It is rarely an unkind stare, or a patronising one, usually a pleasant accepting smile, but it happens. I try to make myself look as nice as possible when I go out with him, knowing we will be looked at, and it makes me feel more confident if my hair is clean, clothes pressed and I am feeling good about myself. Again, I believe parents with Down's syndrome children have to have a protective shell around themselves. I only worry now if I get looked at when I am out without Alex!

Recently Alex and I were travelling to London by tube. Alex knows many of the station names, so I told him which train we would be catching and where we would be changing trains. A very nice older man said, 'I used to work for London Transport. Where do you want to go to, love?' This was very kind, and I am sure that the man would not have approached me if he had not seen Alex. The man's route was definitely the best. We were on a mission to find a shop with plenty of Heavy Metal music, since, sadly, our local one had closed down.

Charlotte had similar encounters with people and Alex, and it is quite obvious that it was very uncomfortable for her, for which we are sorry and sad. Overall Simon, Charlotte and I are very proud of Alex, and his social skills and demeanour, and we love taking him to restaurants and other places.

I must admit that I am not comfortable taking Alex out with another Down's syndrome person if I am the only one in charge. My experience was that two were far more than double trouble. On one occasion, the other child egged Alex on to do something and I felt I was not in control. Also we got more stares. There was an incident when Charlotte and I were incensed by a man looking at us. We retorted quietly, knowing he could not hear, 'Well, you are handicapped, too: you are ugly.' It made us feel a bit better.

One family, after raising four of their own children, started to adopt Down's syndrome children. They had adopted three, because they said how lovely they are. I think this is amazing. We adore Alex, but I would not want to adopt or foster another Down's syndrome person. It is plenty enough with one. Yes, Alex is easy now, and has been for a few years, but it can still be quite challenging as one still needs to look out for him.

Sometimes Mum would look after Alex or Charlotte on their own, and I would take the other one out. It might be for a medical appointment or one of them may be sleeping. I loved taking Charlotte out on her own. I adored the attention she got and the compliments on her clothes and looks. For a short while I felt a 'normal' mum.

Chapter 16

Holiday Experiences

We were determined to take the children to some fun places and have had some memorable holidays. For the first few years, we went to France by car and boat, as I was concerned not to let the children be exposed to too much hot sun. Alex often went up to other families to join in with them, totally uninhibited, and they always seemed welcoming and kind, although it could be embarrassing sometimes. If the families were having a picnic, Alex would sit with them and expect to be fed by them, too.

One year Alex had chicken pox shortly before our holiday. His face was quite spotty, but my father said he would not be contagious, as the scabs had healed over and there was no need to cancel our trip. We did not want people thinking we were irresponsible in taking a child infected with chicken pox on an overnight boat to France—there was no Eurotunnel back then. We tried to minimise Alex being on full show, asking him to sit quietly on a seat. Every time an announcement came over the ship's intercom, it was preceded by a 'bing-bong' noise. Alex found this hilarious and he stood as high as he could on the chair, turning to take in a wide audience, laughing and repeating, 'bing-bong'. People looked around, naturally, and they seemed aghast at his quite poxy face.

As night follows day, we knew Charlotte was almost definitely brewing the chicken pox. Soon after arriving at our holiday cottage, sure enough, poor Charlotte became ill. She suffered so much more than Alex did, and we had a few restless and sleepless nights. A well-meaning French lady enquired, 'Is it the sun that has caused the rash?' I wish I had said 'yes', but, being honest, I said, 'No, chicken pox.' The woman looked as horrified as if I had said 'leprosy'.

When Alex felt better, he ran around on the beach and started rock climbing. We had to watch him because some rocks were really high and jagged, but nothing seemed to deter him.

One day he had diarrhoea as we left the beach. As Alex walked to the car, he was unable to control it and I covered his tracks with sand. We laugh about it now, but Simon was very embarrassed. Luckily, the beach was not crowded. Alex seemed unaware of it as he was quite young. A typical child would at least have given us some warning. There was one positive outcome. Whilst queuing to enter a water park, Alex said, 'I need a loo.' So we were able to by-pass the annoying man with a parrot who had created the queue in the first place, wanting to take our souvenir photo with said bird, at an inflated tourist price.

When Alex and Charlotte were nine and seven, we decided to take them on an aeroplane to Minorca. We had heard how child-friendly Minorca was and this is certainly very true. An older boy of about twelve, called Andrew, befriended us, and in particular Alex. Andrew was a delight. He asked to play with Alex every day, and he tried to help him to swim. He gave Alex a float to use in the water, and Alex did very well with his leg strokes. Charlotte could, of course, swim, but we were determined to get Alex swimming, too. The holiday resort was full of families with young children, and it was a great holiday. I remember spotting a Down's syndrome young man of about twenty, and I had to introduce myself to his father for a chat.

On the flight home, we had taken our shoes off. We put them back on when we landed, and proceeded to the luggage retrieval point. Alex said, 'My foot hurts. There is something in my shoe.' There were lots of people behind us. I said, 'Can you wait a moment?' thinking it was a small stone or something insignificant. He said, 'No.' So we stopped, in the way of everybody, and took his shoe off. It was so funny, although painful for poor Alex, as out fell a Minstrel sweet, about the size of a flat small conker. I had been aware that some children were throwing things fairly harmlessly across the seats in the plane, presumably a Minstrel among them. A typical child would have yelled, 'Mum, there is something big and hard in my shoe and I'm not walking any further!'

I know Charlotte was embarrassed about watching Alex dance at the holiday discos, but you could not stop him dancing. He loves it and dances tirelessly for hours. It is very good exercise, so I have never wanted to discourage him.

One year Alex locked Charlotte in the shed by our holiday cottage. She was not amused, but I thought it was a clever thought process. He knew exactly what he was doing and smiled cheekily.

We had to get up very early to catch the ferry home. We woke the children about five and set off. The next morning, at home, I awoke to find Alex had had terrible diarrhoea. All I could think was, thank goodness this had not happened twenty-four hours earlier, when we were in a rush to leave the holiday cottage. A typical child has fewer gastrointestinal accidents than Alex did, owing to nerve endings and their neurotransmitters.

We once went on a family holiday to France. There was a children's club. As soon as the organisers saw Alex, they had no interest in involving him. Indeed, they looked at me as if I wanted to take a dinosaur into the group. Charlotte didn't want to attend without Alex, so she lost out, too. It was extremely humiliating and embarrassing, but it was not a situation I wanted to challenge, since our precious son was involved.   Happily, at all other holiday children's clubs, Alex and Charlotte were accepted very readily, and they loved going. The leaders always said how well behaved they were. They did all sorts of fun things, such as going on bug hunts and face-painting.

On another family holiday, when Alex was about ten, Alex, Charlotte and I were queuing for the loo. A German man came up to me and, looking at Alex, handed me 200 pesetas for Alex. (This was pre-Euro.) I accepted it with grace, thanking him and looked upon it as a simple kind and generous gesture. Was he just being kind, or did he think, how terrible to have Down's syndrome, I must do something, or sweet child, I must give him something, or unfortunate woman? Some people might take offence but I did not. I could tell the gesture was specifically for Alex and not for Charlotte.

One year we decided to take Alex and Charlotte to America, to Disney World, Florida and to stay with our American ex-neighbours who had moved back to New Jersey. This holiday was shortly after the 9/11 atrocities. We had wondered whether we should still go, and if we were being irresponsible taking two children at that time to the USA. We did go, and fortunately there were no more atrocious events. The airlines were not taking any chances, and frisked both Alex and Charlotte, which Alex found very funny.

Alex loved his small alarm clock, and took it in his back pack. On the way, meandering through the airport corridors to board the plane, a faint ringing was heard. We had no idea it was coming from

Alex's back pack. It seemed that every time he turned a corner, something pressed on his clock and set off the alarm bell.

When Alex and Charlotte were much older, we took them to Las Vegas and other parts of the West Coast. We gave Alex a few dollars to play on the slot machines. After the holiday, when people asked Alex what he liked best, he said 'the gambling'. I hope he did not tell too many people this, especially any health care professionals or social workers. When someone asked Alex if he drank beer, he said he preferred champagne!

We were also lucky enough to take Alex to Graceland in Memphis one year. He had asked to go and he loves Elvis' music. We stayed in the Heartbreak Hotel, and had a wonderful time. We had heard that Elvis had passed away in the toilet, so Alex asked if he could see where it happened, but this was not included in the tour. I honestly think Alex would get maximum points on Mastermind, with Elvis Presley as his specialist subject.

Thus we have had many 'normal' family holidays, and what fun it is, being with both Alex and Charlotte. One of my first thoughts was that Alex would simply follow us round and not interact much, but how wrong I was. Mostly he has behaved perfectly well. We, as a family, have been able to do far more than we ever imagined possible.

Chapter 17

Science and the Future

When I see young couples getting married, so in love, I cannot help but think, please God, let them have normal healthy children. Few people escape the trials, traumas and tribulations of life, but I so wish them not to have a Down's syndrome baby, or indeed a baby with special needs of any kind.

There were some who seemed to delight in telling me how common it is for parents to split up if they have a child with special needs. Even a good friend said this to me. From day one of Alex's life, I doubted Simon and I would part because of the Down's syndrome, but I can see the strain some people go through.

We are often asked if we knew in advance that our first born had Down's syndrome, to which the answer is no. I dread to think what course of action we would have taken, but I really do not think we would have chosen an abortion and, because of our history of infertility, we are so glad we did not know. Initially we had misconceptions of what life would be like with Alex, but he has brought us so much joy and unconditional love and, as a result of that pregnancy and the surgery to deliver him, he paved the way for Charlotte's conception, so he, too, is a wonderful miracle.

Science progresses all the time, and we hear regularly about new tests being developed to detect Down's syndrome in pregnant women. We could not be without Alex and never wish we did not have him. We feel that he is fulfilled, but it is the parents who have the anxiety and sadness, and I am sure this is the case for most, if not all, parents of Down's syndrome children. It is one thing to consider the possibility of being without a person you already know, but totally different considering the prevention of Down's syndrome babies being born in the future. We know nothing can stop Down's syndrome from arising at conception, but people can decide if they want to proceed with their pregnancy, albeit making for a sad and painful situation. While this will touch some nerves and abortion is a controversial subject, it is my belief that if Down's syndrome can be detected very early on, this can only be a good thing. Couples can then decide if they want to proceed with their pregnancy or, however sad, they can choose to abort before the baby has had a chance to develop beyond early growth. Anyone who feels really strongly about abortion could decline the tests. More tests are available now than twenty-seven years ago. There are non-invasive blood tests, for example. My first scan was carried out at sixteen weeks gestation, which was the normal practice back then.

We were lucky, Alex is healthy, but many Down's syndrome babies have health problems, in particular heart or gastric conditions. This is terrible for the parents and baby to endure, often needing many hospital procedures and admissions.

We cannot over-emphasize how Alex has enriched our lives, how endearing and loving he is. He is so warm, extremely humorous, and unconditional love pours from him. He is always eager to please, and he adores all the family. He says, 'Take care of yourself,' to his grandmothers, and many other caring things. Sometimes I say 'silly me' if I drop something and he always says, 'Mum, you are beautiful', and he means it. One day, I overreacted when Alex opened the dishwasher door whilst in use, and exclaimed, 'ALEX!' He was so upset. 'Sorry, Mum,' he said. I felt really bad but when the same thing happened with Charlotte as perpetrator, she grunted, 'So?' a normal teenage reaction.

Another time, I was walking near our house when Alex saw me. He ran excitedly and exclaimed, 'I saw my beautiful Mum!' My sister-in-law said, 'Oh yes, what is he after!' but I can say with absolute certainty that it was a genuine affectionate comment without any ulterior motive.

In essence, much as we love Alex and could not contemplate eradicating him, but to prevent Down's syndrome babies being born in future is, to my mind, progress. This may sound harsh, but I do not want other couples to experience the pain of the early years, and the on-going worries for the future. Sometimes people say things such as 'Down's syndrome people teach you so much about life and people', but why should my son have to endure Down's syndrome and its associated developmental delay, the physical characteristics, the limitations imposed upon him, the limited opportunities and possible hardships, just to teach others about life?

When we were told by the paediatrician that if you have to have a child with special needs, Down's syndrome is the best disability to have, this has proved to be quite true. Most Down's syndrome people can walk, talk, run, swim, read and write and do a host of other things. In short, we believe we have had a fairly 'normal' life. Alex has not stopped us doing anything or going anywhere we wanted to, apart from maybe skiing, but I am not sure I wanted to try that! I met a mother once who said, 'You are so good. You take Alex everywhere and go on all ordinary family outings.' We never contemplated not doing these things, apart from during the very early days. Our aim was to carry on as normally as possible and bring Alex up as we would Charlotte or any other child.

I do not want to upset anyone with a child with a disability other than Down's syndrome and who is unable to do some of the above mentioned tasks, but, as I have mentioned, my own experience is limited to having a child with Down's syndrome, which is what I wanted to write about. I am not at all qualified to discuss other disabilities and I do not pretend to have any idea of what other people may have to go through.

When I hear that someone has miscarried, naturally I feel sad for them, and of course you know how devastated the parents must be. There are many reasons for miscarriage, many that cannot be explained by doctors yet. However, taking a scientific view, we know this may be nature's way of eradicating an unhealthy foetus. Since having Alex, I always wonder if someone's miscarriage was for the best, but, without fully knowing the cause, this is little comfort to the would-be mother. I cannot help thinking that possibly the prospective parents have been saved from having a child with considerable special needs.

Chapter 18

Food for Thought

Naturally, there are moments, maybe hours, when a new parent of a Down's syndrome baby feels utter desolation, despair and sadness. In my experience, this is usually short lived, because life is so busy and has to go on. Food has to be bought and cooked and the house has to be run, husbands organised, considered and cared for, too. The innocent baby needs caring for and he/she has no idea what pain they may have brought you, which, though sad, is not their fault. This knowledge is one of the main things which kept us going. I also remember thinking how terrible Down's syndrome is. I thought of other traumas such as bereavement, alcoholism, redundancies, and so on where time may help you to cope or change some of these situations, but with Down's syndrome the extra chromosome will always be there. I am sure other new parents will have had the same thoughts.

If and when you feel like this, it is sometimes helpful to consider situations far worse. I think it may help you. Thinking that there is someone far worse off may be a little selfish, but it is so true. When Alex was first born, I looked at people out and about in the street, laughing and enjoying themselves. I wanted to ask, 'Don't you know what has happened? Why is the sun still shining and the birds still singing?'

I remember one particular day, when Alex was a few months old, feeling distraught. Then I heard the news that there had been a fire at King's Cross station, killing thirty-one innocent people. It brought me to my senses, and made me stop wallowing in our own family sadness. Sadly, atrocities happen all the time and we cannot control or stop them. While one doesn't think, 'that's all right, then, these things are far worse', it does give a sense of perspective for the desolate moments, which, mercifully, become fewer as time goes on.

Soon after Charlotte was born, in April 1989, there was the Monkseaton massacre, killing innocent people. Then, in 2001, there was 9/11.

My sister, Diane, lost her beautiful twenty-six-year-old daughter in a road accident in 2003. Although I said at the beginning of this book that to have a child with Down's syndrome feels as if you have lost your child, this is transient and there can be no comparison with my sister's grief.

A distant relative, Aunty Mim, lost her twenty-eight-year-old son, also in a road accident, when Charlotte was about six months old. We went to see her and I do hope I was not tactless when I told her that we felt we had lost our son when he was born, because we were grieving for a typical baby, to which she said, 'But you've still got him, haven't you?'

As mentioned earlier, I hate the fact Down's syndrome people stand out. I am always surprised how really young children soon see or pick up that Alex is different, and sometimes ask questions or stare at him. I recently noticed a very young child of about four on the tube staring questioningly at Alex, presumably because of the facial characteristics.

On one family holiday in Minorca, a family arrived after us with a slim, good-looking twenty-year-old son and a pretty fourteen-year-old daughter. The young man went to the top of the diving board and sat down, making some strange noises. It soon became obvious that he had special needs. We became friendly with the family after meeting on an excursion. The mother and I went on a shopping trip during which we had a good heart-to-heart conversation. She told me how uncomfortable it could be when people looked at her son because of his behavioural problems, because he looked totally typical. She thought that having a Down's syndrome youngster was much better than someone like her son, because everybody can see the Down's instantly and therefore be more accepting of any unusual behaviour.

Chapter 19

Thoughts and Incidents

I can't say when the acceptance of the Down's syndrome happened for us. The night before any of Alex's birthdays has always been a really difficult time for me, none more so than the night before his first birthday. I felt really sad. This is because you think back to a year ago, or however many years have passed, and you remember how you felt: the joy, excitement and anticipation of soon becoming a mother, especially after such a long wait for this happiness, totally unaware of what was to follow. It is much the same after a bereavement. Six days afterwards one thinks, this time last week, everything was fine, and we still had our loved one.

This sadness before each birthday did last a few years, even if it was also really hectic organising cakes, parties, not forgetting the party bags, and various celebrations. Milestone birthdays like eighteen and twenty-one are also bittersweet. We are happy and Alex is always really excited and happy, but I can't help thinking, what if? I am not down for long, though, and join in the fun to give Alex a memorable, happy birthday and thanking goodness I became a mother. Probably the night before Alex's thirtieth birthday is going to be particularly painful, too, since it is another milestone birthday.

Whenever I hear that a new Down's syndrome baby has been born I feel incredibly sad and usually cry. I cannot help but feel for the new parents and their bewilderment, knowing what they are going through and how they must be feeling. It always brings back our raw and despairing memories, but I do hope this book can help and give reassurance.

I often think back to those early days, and how excited and elated Simon and I were, and how this was so severely quashed after Alex's delivery.

It's strange how we count our blessings. A friend told me that one of her friends had multiple sclerosis (MS). This person had a young daughter. The MS had not progressed too far, but on a bad day she could only drag one leg behind her when walking. I thought how sad and worrying as the mother of a very young child, to have such a disease. This mother did not know that I knew she had MS. Talking to me at a child's birthday party, she was very sweet. She asked me how I coped, having a Down's syndrome baby. Privately, I thought, how do you cope with MS? To me, that was far worse. To her, having a Down's syndrome baby was evidently worse than her problem.

When Alex was about four, he had to have an adenoidectomy. We had to be admitted to the hospital the day before the operation. Alex was particularly lively and running around. It was really hard to keep him occupied. There was a playroom and playroom assistant, with all sorts of paints and books and activities which was open for most of the day. I kept Alex occupied as best I could, but the playroom/nursery nurse had absolutely no intention of helping out, which was her job. She only helped the typical children. I know I should have asked or even complained, but it can be very hard on a mother; you don't want to make it look like you need help, cannot cope or want sympathy, as it brings attention to the situation.

One of the mothers was a widow, waiting for her very young son to have a heart transplant. That put me in my place in that I realised how much better our situation was.

I read recently about an autistic child who mostly behaved well but who had terrible outbursts of aggression, suddenly and without warning attacking his mother. I again counted my blessings. The mother said she wished she could put him down. I can totally understand this. Although I would never have harmed Alex, during challenging moments, which I am sure were due to his frustration at being unable to communicate his thoughts during the early years, I often thought about what I might do out of desperation on the spur of the moment. I think every mother has had those thoughts. I rehearsed what I would say to the judge in court. That's how desperate I was. Don't misunderstand this: I would never have done anything to Alex, but such thoughts arise when behaviour gets out of control.

When Alex was about four, a well-known newspaper invited people to write about a moment which changed their lives forever. I started to write about Alex and duly sent the article off. I said I wanted it to be anonymous, which I think shows that I had not accepted the Down's syndrome then. I was not ready for people at work and others to read about us, should it be printed. The newspaper contacted me and I was told that they would like to print my article but would have to use our names. I declined, but kept the article. Now I am ready to share our story, hopefully to help and encourage other families in a similar situation. Clearly, we have now accepted the Down's syndrome and not just Alex since I wrote that article.

I said earlier that I wished we had not known about the Down's syndrome straight away, but retrospectively I know that was unwise. I read recently about a woman who did not know her son had Down's syndrome until he was two. This is almost unbelievable and must have been a greater shock than finding out at birth.

Many years ago, my father had a family in his practice, where the only child, a boy, was disabled, in a wheelchair. I do not know what was wrong with him. His parents never took him further than the back garden. That is so awfully sad. I don't know if they were ashamed of their son, or did not want him stared at or it may have been because of practical difficulties. When the parents grew older, their son went into a home, where he was so happy to be with similar young adults.

This happened to many families years ago, since disabled people were excluded from society. Even in the twenty-six years since Alex was born, attitudes have changed and disabled children and adults are now very much included in modern society.

Down's syndrome is supposed to be fairly rare. Indeed, many family doctors may not have come across any patients with Down's syndrome. When Alex was born, there were a few Down's syndrome babies born in the area at the same time. It was as if there was a cluster of the condition, which makes me wonder if anything could have led to this genetic accident. A statistician would say it was a statistical quirk, but I often ponder this. Having said that Down's syndrome is fairly rare, two unrelated friends of ours know three families with Down's syndrome children of differing ages, where there is no connection at all between any of these families.

My social worker put me in touch with other mothers with Down's syndrome babies in the area, and we became friends. They say that a problem shared is a problem halved and it was, and still is, very therapeutic to meet up with these mothers and compare and share information and, above all, to have a laugh whilst supporting each other. We still meet up, even if not often enough.

One of our friends has a child with special needs. It was not diagnosed until the child was about two. This was twenty years ago, and the paediatricians could not say exactly what the problem was, so this child has no specific label. This is so hard for the parents as they have no one with whom to discuss the condition on a scientific level and no guidance on what to expect or how the condition may manifest itself, nor any idea of the cause.

I believe in fate and I have an uncanny coincidence to share. After a baby is born, you have six weeks in which to register the birth, usually between nine and four pm. I went to register Alex's birth quite late into the six weeks. Unbeknown to me, a Down's syndrome baby girl had been born at Northwick Park Hospital on June 19th, which was nineteen days after Alex's birth. Bearing in mind the mother, Janet, had almost three weeks after me to register her baby girl's birth, we had gone at exactly the same time to register our baby's names. We recognised each other from an antenatal class. I had Alex with me, but Janet was on her own. I had not accepted the Down's syndrome then, but for some reason I said that Alex had Down's syndrome. It is almost unbelievable but Janet replied that her baby, Joanna, also had Down's syndrome.

To us, this was a really strange coincidence of timings and circumstances, and must have been meant to be. We exchanged phone numbers and became friends almost immediately. In many ways, we were very alike and we knew we would be friends, with or without the Down's syndrome connection. We took the children on holidays to Euro Disney and on many outings and frequently met up. Alex and Joanna were friends and Charlotte was friendly with Janet's other daughter, Samantha. We helped each other to cope with the shock and other problems. It seemed that if Janet was down, I could cheer her up and vice versa. Very sadly, Janet died about eight years ago.

Another not so strange coincidence happened when my father did a locum for a local doctor. A friend of mine had a Down's syndrome baby who was ill. She took the baby to her surgery and happened to see my father, not knowing he was my father. She was very protective and said, 'He has got Down's syndrome.' My father, sweet as always, said, 'My dear, I have seven grandchildren, one with and six without Down's syndrome, so I know how you are feeling.' The mother could not wait to tell me how caring, kind and understanding my father had been, as she then realised the connection.

Chapter 20

Support

For any new mothers of a Down's syndrome baby, there will always be days when you just want to look after your baby and not be thinking about Down's syndrome and the associated problems, but it is important to ask for a social worker if you have not been assigned one. With luck, he/she will not be as annoying as ours. Well-meaning and nice as she was, she had a very irritating habit of putting her head on one side in an overly dramatic way, intended to convey compassion and sympathy. Sometimes we just couldn't take it, becoming hostile to the sympathy and the compassionate voice. I know it is well meant, and I know I must have seemed ungrateful, but that is how it is sometimes. One does not necessarily want sympathy or to open up to a stranger. I remember our social worker mentioning a respite home where Alex could stay sometimes. This was really meant with kindness, but we did not feel we needed respite, since our parents helped out a lot. I repeated to my parents what she had said. My father, tongue in cheek, said, 'Tell her you know a respite home for alcoholic social workers.' Though illogical, it made me smile.

Another social worker turned up at my hospital bedside within days of Alex's birth, always when I was about to feed him or take a shower. Somehow I did not warm to her and I found it too soon, so annoying and upsetting as I wasn't ready. There is a time and place, after all, and it would have been helpful to have agreed some later visits.

The social worker should give advice about what is available in your area, what help you are entitled to and reassure you that you are not alone. Everybody copes slightly differently. You may want masses of information immediately, or you may prefer to wait awhile. I also suggest speaking with and perhaps joining The Down's Syndrome Association (DSA) telephone 0333 1212 300 http://www.downs-syndrome.org.uk/

They can give you invaluable support and advice, so there is no need to suffer alone, which, as I know only too well, can happen in those painful first days. You will, if possible, be put in touch with other mothers in your area with Down's syndrome children. My friends and I formed a group called ACTA (A Chance To Achieve) in our Borough of Hillingdon for Down's syndrome mothers.

I was recently asked if I felt attitudes have changed towards people with Down's syndrome. I am pleased to say that I have nearly always been pleasantly surprised by the lack of prejudice I have encountered, and have rarely experienced nasty staring looks and comments, as I had anticipated soon after Alex's birth. One thing is certain though, attitudes may have changed towards Down's syndrome but the desolate feelings of the parents have not.

I was disappointed though, to hear from a mother about an outdated/uneducated remark by an Ear, Nose and Throat consultant. The consultant apparently made a comment to the effect that improving the child's hearing would add nothing to the child's learning abilities. We were astounded by this. To be fair to this consultant, who is now about ninety years old, the comment was made many years ago and it is likely that this may have been the general feeling at the time. Over the last forty years, society has definitely realised the possible potential of Down's syndrome people, thanks to the Down's Syndrome Association and general publicity. I am therefore glad for Alex that he is only twenty-six, since he has had more support and input than he would have done in the past.

As with anybody, there is a range of abilities of typical people and equally a range of abilities with Down's syndrome people. Some Down's syndrome people are lucky and have extensive educational, social and behavioural input, and some do not. All the Down's syndrome people I know show a range of individual skills, from cooking, cycling, shopping, travelling alone, and many more.

Alex was very lucky. We had Portage, as described earlier, Ingrid as a learning support assistant, and the local college whose student nurses did family placements with us. That was great. Overall we had about fifteen nurses over the years, who generally were extremely helpful to us and grateful for the experience, so it was a real symbiotic relationship. One of these nurses taught Alex to tell the time. In fact, most people gave overwhelming support.

A real risk is that of holding your child back. We did not want to wrap Alex in cotton wool and cosset him, but on the other hand, he certainly is more vulnerable than a non-Down's syndrome person.

There is no doubt that we could have let go sooner over some things, like his mobile phone. He uses a smart phone so well now. Too well, in fact! Mind you, you could say he did not need one as a teenager since he was never out alone, but many of his friends had them. He is constantly texting and phoning. We are trying to address this with him. Most people are busy and do not want to receive so many texts. If he doesn't receive a reply within a short space of time, the same message is re-sent. People have said, 'I don't mind, but Alex phoned me ten times last week.' Most of our friends and relatives are understanding, but it is embarrassing.

Alex is so affectionate and he may say things like, 'Night, night, sleep well, love you and thinking of you.' I know he doesn't mean it romantically, but we have had people saying that Alex is sending them inappropriate texts. I found this upsetting and I asked him not to text them again, ever. I know I am being defensive, but it is extremely hard to accept Alex's ways sometimes. I recently told him that he was addicted to texting and it must stop, to which he replied, 'Describe what addicted means, please.'

Alex had a great, caring friend from a local group, Dimensions, called Roz, who cooked with him, took him out and did some travel training. I had not thought it possible for Alex to travel alone by bus to a local town, but he can do so now, thanks to Roz's perseverance. First they travelled together on the bus, enforcing and re-enforcing the route, where the bus stops were, how to sit near the driver and other safety matters. This they did a few times together. Then they travelled the same route, but with Alex going 'alone' in front, with Roz following closely behind. When Roz was satisfied Alex knew exactly what to do, and Alex also felt comfortable with the journey, he used to meet Roz in the town. He then suggested they met in Starbucks, with Alex ordering his own drink and waiting for Roz. The first time Alex went alone on the bus, one light evening, you can imagine how Simon and I waited nervously for him to text us announcing his safe arrival before meeting up with a supervised group. Then Alex texted to say he was coming back after being put on the bus, which had us waiting anxiously at the door. He was so proud, and so were we. The trouble is, whilst the above training is amazing, we are relying on normal bus services, and any deviations can cause problems, because Alex would not, for instance, know an alternative route home, but at least we can be in touch by mobile phone. One day Alex was coming back from my mother's house and he waited nearly an hour for a bus in the cold. Luckily, he had the sense to walk back to my mother's and phone us. Roz definitely gave Alex more confidence and encouragement to do things. She knew he could do it and she treated him wonderfully. Being the mother of four grown-up girls meant she was very experienced in dealing with children and young adults.

As his mother, I think I spoilt him and worried about his capabilities. It is difficult, though, because we may think Alex understands something, but then he surprises us by asking a question, making it obvious he has not understood what we have said. For instance, Alex loves Elvis Presley and Heavy Metal—in fact most music. One of Elvis's songs is called 'A Little Less Conversation', which we talk about with him. One day when Alex was talking non-stop, Simon said to him, 'How about a little less conversation?' Alex replied, 'What does that mean, Dad?' Confused, we tried to explain, but wonder if he ever understood the meaning of the words.

We know a boy with undiagnosed special needs, who appears a typical young adult, until you get to know him. He was being assessed by a social worker. This boy told the social worker that he wanted to be a journalist. The social worker thought he came across as perfectly normal. Soon after, the boy said, 'What is a journalist?' This demonstrates the predicament of knowing when someone properly understands the language they are using. We always bear this in mind with conversations with Alex.

Alex is not very good with money. It is hard for him to grasp the maths, so he is unsure of what change he should have. Once I gave him £20 to go for his haircut 'all by himself'. It should have cost about £12, and I told him to leave a £1 tip. He came back with £2. I could not get a straight answer out of him about the missing £5. I overreacted, because we know the barber shop and staff very well indeed and I was sure Alex would not lie to me. Whilst I was absolutely sure that the barber would not give Alex the wrong change, I marched to the barber's shop. The owner, a dear lady, looked surprised to see me and immediately asked if there was anything wrong. I explained about the money. She said, 'I am positive I gave Alex the correct change, especially as I have just checked and balanced the till. But it's only a fiver, so please have £5.' I took it and thanked her, wondering who was right. Later on that evening, Alex produced £5 from his pocket. I was mortified. On cross-examination, Alex, needless to say, had no straight answers. I think it must have been the barber's money. I went to the barber shop as soon as I could and explained, returning the £5.

It is tough watching much younger family members and children of friends developing and learning typically, achieving good reading, writing and spelling, highlighting the vast difference in ability between them and Alex. My great nieces can write better stories than Alex can, and naturally Charlotte's school progress surpassed Alex's straight away.

Potty training was a particular challenge, but when mastered, it is so rewarding. One always meets these annoying mothers who delight in telling you how their little Johnny, who is destined to be an Oxford professor, was potty trained at nine months or whatever. One hears these comments whether you have a special needs baby or not. These mothers think it is a sign of intelligence to potty train early, but it is not. It is all to do with nerve impulses from the bladder or bowel to the brain. Just as typical children may walk at any time from ten months or two years, it is not related to intelligence. We mothers are proud of all our children's accomplishments, but I could have done without these women telling me about Little Johnny's amazing bladder control. I tried not to dwell on other typical children and their speed at learning and general progression and awareness, for it always caused some heartache.

There is great joy when your Down's syndrome baby/child learns something new. Usually you have had to put in a lot of extra effort, hence I always feel it is extra rewarding.

Once, on holiday in Italy, Alex and I had been having fun in the swimming pool. Later, a lady came up to me and said, 'I was watching you and your son in the swimming pool. He really loves you, doesn't he?' You never know who is watching you!

Alex, and I believe this is a common trait of Down's syndrome, has slight obsessive compulsive disorder (OCD) tendencies. For instance, he always likes to use a blue cup, and since watching 'Home Alone' as a young boy, always 'spread-eagles' his pyjamas on his bed just like Macaulay Culkin in the film. He also lays his deodorants and aftershave out in a particular order on his chest of drawers, and if they get moved, he immediately puts them back to how they were. This is not a problem to him or us. He doesn't get angry, he just likes things 'just so', and remembers his preferred lay-out. In a way this is a positive trait, since he rarely loses things. I assume these tendencies help him locate his belongings. I heard recently from a mother of a Cambridge graduate son that she has lost count of the number of times her son phones her having lost his phone/keys/bank card, or requesting that she courier his phone charger or whatever immediately!

Many people have similar OCD tendencies, so it is nothing to worry about. I myself like to put pound notes in my wallet facing the same way, and when filling the car with petrol, I have to stop at a round number of pounds and pence.

Since writing this, Alex has dropped his phone in the loo, which doesn't bear thinking about. I was desperate when the staff in his hostel phoned to tell me, because I know how he is almost obsessed with texting all the family and friends. I knew he would be lost without it. We asked him to store it in uncooked rice overnight, which can absorb the moisture, but this didn't work. A new phone was soon purchased. Luckily, he coped very well in the meantime, emailing instead. Charlotte and some others were slightly relieved, because they knew the texts from Alex would diminish for a while. In fact Charlotte said 'Result!' which hurt me. I know she was joking, but the maternal instinct kicked in. I had hoped, though, that it would have curbed his desire to text almost constantly, when he is relaxing.

He emailed me, saying he 'felt sad today'. I know it was because he felt bereft without a phone. I was really upset since he had never said that before. True, this is a normal maternal reaction to any child saying such things, but nevertheless, it is compounded by the Down's syndrome and the fact that he cannot always easily explain his feelings. His level of communication is obviously different from a typical child. Thank goodness he can tell us most things, though, like if someone is bullying him, being unkind or stealing from him. I remember one of Alex's friends who could not speak, and I was so upset for his mother. This boy also went to a residential college. Imagine his poor mother not being able to tell for sure how happy he was, or ask him anything. We are eternally grateful we can communicate with Alex. He absorbs everything we talk about, and we have to be careful about what he may repeat, since he does not understand tact and timing. For instance, over dinner at a family wedding, Alex told my cousin that our cat had worms. Things like that make us laugh and are inconsequential, but we are careful what we choose to say in front of him.

Chapter 21

Overview

There we have it, the story of our wonderful, adorable Alex, from infertility to pregnancy, a terrible shock, a miracle Charlotte and our love for them both.

We would not change him for the world, but so wish he did not have Down's syndrome. He is so loving and sweet, kind and considerate. A friend asked me to add what impeccable manners Alex has. He can Skype me now, sometimes after his shower, before getting dressed. Luckily, I can only see his face and chest. I smile at his innocence of such situations.

Once I asked him if he wanted us to take him anything while visiting him in Birmingham. I thought he might say coca cola or chocolate. His reply was, 'Just a few toilet rolls.'

We don't know how much he realises he is different and it is not easy to discuss this with him. He did ask why he did not have a car, since Charlotte did. I believe that if you asked him if he wanted to drive today, he would say yes, assuming he would be able to.

He is such a jolly person to have around. Also, his thought processes never cease to amaze us. When he was about six, he had some sweets. I asked him to share them with a friend of mine, Celia. Alex said, 'No, Celia's on a diet.' I thought this was very clever and logical, if not typically selfish of a child wanting to keep the sweets to himself.

Unfortunately, our dear Aunty Megs developed dementia and was cared for in a home. We went to see her during a Christmas concert. She had been wheeled into the room to watch the concert, but by this time she was in a vegetative state. When we later arrived home and I mentioned her name to Simon, Alex enquired if that was the lady who was 'dead'. He had assumed that as Aunty neither spoke nor moved, she was not alive.

Another time, we were discussing relatives who might get married after cousin Ben married. It was all to do with weight, since Alex had purposely lost weight for Ben's wedding. I suggested he kept his weight down, in case we had another family wedding. He asked, 'Who else might get married?' I said Kate and Zoe may marry. They are two sisters. I should have said, 'Kate OR Zoe may get married.' Alex exclaimed, 'Don't be silly! They are sisters.'

Alex once asked Simon, 'If hamburgers come from Hamburg, where do cheeseburgers come from?'

My father often took Alex for a haircut. My father would read the newspaper whilst waiting. One day, Alex asked the barber to shave his head, to look like his art teacher, whom Alex hero-worshipped. My father had no idea of Alex's request. My father and I were very laid back about it, and thought it was very amusing, but my mother, Simon and Charlotte were horrified. I thought it was nice that Alex had consciously thought about it and been able to ask for it. After all, hair does re-grow.

Sometimes we bought a sausage sandwich from a café we regularly used, usually as a take-away wrapped in a disposable box. Alex asked if he could go and buy it 'all by myself'. I gave him the money and off he went proudly. On his return to our agreed meeting point, in the shopping mall, I didn't know whether to laugh or cry. Alex came carefully through the mall clutching his sandwich on the café's plate, as I had not thought to remind him to ask for a take-away. We brought it home and I returned the plate on our next visit, saying, 'This is your plate and please don't ask how I came to have it.' Looking at Alex, they simply smiled.

One day we had one of Alex's friends to tea. When I was about to take the friend home, I told the three young children, 'Stand at the front door, please. Have you all got shoes and coats on?' this being the usual process for my little ones. I asked Alex to pick up the yellow supermarket bag which contained a video tape we had borrowed from this particular friend. About a week later, the friend's mother phoned up and asked, 'Is there any reason why Johnny brought home a pair of muddy football boots?' We laughed. Somehow the video bag had been muddled with Charlotte's football boots. I had not checked what was being returned.

Alex has an amazing memory and sense of humour. He remembers all the birthdays of friends and family, rattles them off and is always reminding me by text of someone's birthday. We also discovered by chance that if you ask Alex what day of the week various dates had fallen on, he would know instantly, even going back a year. He appears to have a photographic memory of the calendar. He loves comedy programmes like 'Only Fools and Horses' (laughing at his grandfather, who called it 'Old Fools and Horses') Fawlty Towers, Laurel and Hardy and many more. Once we walked past a pub playing an 'Only Fools and Horses' episode, and after hearing one line, he remarked, 'That was the Rodney Come Home story,' which Simon verified as correct.

When I was growing up, I clearly remember telling my father about various problems; he was always so encouraging and did his best to minimize any worries. He often said, 'It's not the end of the world,' and that does put things in perspective. I must use this phrase often with our children, too, because when I ticked Alex off for texting me the same words about five times, he retorted, 'It's not the end of the world, Mum,' which made me smile and it was hard to reprimand him further.

Chapter 22

Friends and Family

I have tried to ask friends and family how they felt when they heard about Alex's diagnosis, but I am not sure they would necessarily tell me exactly how they felt. I think they must have just felt very sad and grateful it had not happened to them. My mother said she knew very little about Down's syndrome since she had never come across it before. She fully remembers my father receiving a telephone call whilst sitting with friends around the dinner table, soon after Alex's birth. Dad left the room and was extremely quiet and upset. Apparently the call had been from the paediatrician, Dr Lieberman. Presumably it was confirmation of the Down's syndrome.

Some friends were not sure whether to include us in certain social gatherings. They did include us in parties for children and so on, but it is interesting that it crossed their minds as to whether it was a good idea or not.

Some friends who became pregnant soon after had amniocentesis carried out. Whilst I fully agreed with their course of action, after all, we all listen to friends and read newspapers, watch television and learn from other people's experiences, it does make you feel odd to hear about it. It is difficult to explain, because you definitely do not want them to go through what you have done, but I felt hurt and wished they had not told me they were having the test. I felt they were saying, 'We do not want a Down's syndrome baby like you,' which I understand, but would rather not think about. One friend said, 'I had an amniocentesis because we certainly did not want a Down's syndrome baby.'

An aunt asked us if Alex would ever walk and a colleague remarked, 'I think Alex is a good one.' Good what, I thought. Martian? I know she meant Alex seemed more able than other children with Down's syndrome and she thought it was a compliment, but I was upset.

A family friend's grandmother looked at baby Alex, then looked at me and said, 'Shame, innit, but he'll grow out of it, won't he?'

I kept the letters that friends and family wrote to me when they heard about Alex's diagnosis after his birth. They are sweet and supportive, expressing their shock and surprise. Re-reading them takes me back to the dark days of despair, but they are a comfort, knowing that we had such kind friends and family and that we have managed to overcome the negatives and been a very happy family with love, determination and support.

Some of the comments over the years have made us laugh, cry or simply baffled us. They have sometimes been a real slap in the face, but we like to think they are to the consequence of ignorance and not meant to hurt.

Once over dinner at our house, an elderly relative remarked, 'Is he having speech therapy, because I cannot understand a word he is saying?' I was very cross. They were eating our food, drinking our wine at our table, with our darling Alex. I know elderly people often lose their tact, but really, in front of him . . .

I do wonder if any family members or friends are embarrassed by Alex. I do not feel I can ask them, and I doubt they could say yes anyway. However, when our nephew, Ben, married Nikki, he asked Alex to be an usher, which was wonderful. This meant so much to us, especially Alex, and was appreciated greatly. This confirmed how Alex was loved and accepted by the family.

It is also difficult to tell family and friends how much they mean to Alex, and of course they have their own families to look after. Alex wants to see the family and our friends as often as possible, and I explain it is not always possible because of work, their own family life and geographic constraints. I know he finds this hard to understand and deal with, especially as he hero-worships his cousins, particularly the male ones. He copies them by pretending to like beer, 'supports' Chelsea Football Club and loves to go out with them since he looks up to them with great regard. They are his role models.

Recently I asked a friend if we could call in as Alex wanted to see her. She was not feeling well and asked if we could wait until Alex next came home, which I understood, but Alex was upset since he would not be coming home again for about eight weeks.

We have been particularly friendly with a local family since Alex and Charlotte were at playschool. One of the girls is the same age as Alex, and she was having a 21st birthday party. They had been in the same class in primary school for a while. Charlotte was asked to the party, but not Alex. After a couple of glasses of wine while out with the mother, a good friend, I cried and said that I understood why Alex was not invited, but it was so sad. The mother very kindly said that Alex could go, she would be there and could watch out for him. Charlotte got upset and said, 'Please, Mum, no. He will be so embarrassing, break dancing all evening.' I did not pursue it in case the hostess was embarrassed and, although I felt bad about it, we told Alex it was a girls' party.

My father had and my mother still has a very close relationship with Alex, as with all their grandchildren. When my father passed away, all the grandchildren said a few words each at a Memorial

Service. Charlotte asked Alex to write something about 'Dadda'. Alex wrote this totally by himself:

> HELLO I want to say about
> MY Grandad Dadda.
>
> MY Grandad he has been
> a nice Man to look after
> and he has been given his
> Grandchildren money for birthdays
> and christmas.
>
> Dadda has been a nice *wonderful young*
> Man and he had three Daughters
> and beautiful wife called Nanna Phil.
> Dadda Loved having Friends
> and he almost liked John and Pam.
> Dadda Loved taking Nanna, and Myself
> and charlotte to see My *Fair* Lady
> and he Loved watching Fairy Lady
> On the dvd Player and *Dadda Loved* my Fairy Lady
> sitting on his chair sleeping all afternoon.

'Hello, I want to say about my Granddad Dadda.

My Granddad, he has been a nice man to look after and he has been giving his grandchildren money for birthdays and Christmas.

Dadda has been a nice wonderful young man and he had three daughters and beautiful wife called Nanna Phyll.

Dadda loved having friends and he also liked John and Pam.

Dadda loved taking Nanna and myself and Charlotte to see My Fair Lady at the theatre and he loved watching My Fair Lady on the DVD player and Dadda loved sitting on his chair sleeping all afternoon.'

We were greatly comforted by all the grandchildren's memories and choked by Alex's little speech. Not only was our father a loving father and grandfather, but he was an eminent doctor who was highly thought of by his patients and peers, as we were repeatedly told.

*

Since starting this book, two nieces have given birth for the first time, to Oscar and Wesley, who are beautiful baby boys. I cuddled them and shared the parents' elation. I did not think, if only Alex did not have Down's syndrome, for once, but instead I thanked God for the babies and their parents, that they had a safe delivery of a typical gorgeous baby each, such a precious gift. I know the love they feel for their new babies and am glad that they have no idea how devastating it was for us to find out about Alex's Down's syndrome.

My mother has become very frail and, at age ninety-two, she has decided to go into a nursing home. I suggested she move in with Simon and me. Simon really did not mind if she did, but she said, 'No, it would not be fair on you both. You have extra responsibilities with Alex and I would not dream of you looking after me.' We were very touched.

Charlotte says she feels guilty about not seeing Alex more often and doing more for him. We tell her that it is not her responsibility to care for him or to worry unduly about him, which she knows, but she loves him very much and has accepted the Down's syndrome. She wishes she could look after him, but she has a good job and we want her to have her own life. I would say it is only recently that she has been able to accept him completely, which is fine. Charlotte readily invites Alex to the cinema or to stay with her and her boyfriend now. Alex adores them both and he is extremely happy to go out with them. As parents we love Alex and care for him unquestioningly, but it is very different for siblings to come to terms with and accept their atypical sibling, especially as they don't usually have any friends with the same situation.

Moving on !

My name is Alex and I learnt how to travel on my own !
I did travel training with Hillingdon Outreach and my support worker, Roz, helped me not to be scared. Being able to go places on my own meant that I did not have to ask mum and dad for a lift all the time and I could meet up at Uxbridge station and go on trips with everyone like the cinema, fish & chips, harvester, London, or bowling and have lots of fun .
I could also go and see my Nan for a cup of tea and cake by myself.
I do not live at home any more and have moved to Birmingham so I have to learn where all the new buses go but I am not scared now as I know I can do it .
If you have not been on a bus or train on your own then ask them to help you too.

Excerpt from Alex

When Alex was ten and a half years old, the tutor of the Special Needs nurses asked me if I could write a short piece about life with Alex. This same tutor asked if I could repeat this when Alex was seventeen. It is interesting, historically, to read my views at these points and to see how life has changed. Some of the content is a repeat of what I have already said earlier in the book, but I did not want to omit these thoughts from those times. The extracts highlight how much better and easier life became with time.

1.   Alex at age 10.5, February 1998

We love our little boy, who is now aged 10.5, with Down's syndrome, but life is not easy, although it is much better now than it used to be. There are times when you want to pull your hair out, but I realise that all mums feel this at some time or other.

When I feel really low, I stop and think that it's not his fault he is handicapped and that he would far rather be normal.

At first you think you feel as though your baby has died, because you are in such a state of shock, and you are mourning the anticipated healthy normal child that you had hoped for.

I think it takes a long time to come to terms with this, although everybody differs in the way they cope with situations.

Our baby was lovely, very contented and easy, and we bonded easily, but we were so upset that he had Down's syndrome.

He took a long time to potty train and I found it stressful when he had accidents when he was older, even at about 4 years plus, since it was rare for other children to have accidents at that age. Also, if he does something wrong or behaves badly when out with friends or in public places, I find it very hard. I think it is much worse than if an 'ordinary' child does something wrong, because you feel everyone is thinking, 'poor mother', and how terrible it must be to have a handicapped child.

When he was little, I regularly came home in tears as I just could not cope with him sometimes. For instance, once he pushed a little girl down some stairs. The mother, my good friend, was very good about it, but I was so ashamed; after all, he could have broken the little girl's neck. Another time, in a playground, a mother called out, 'Is that your boy, because he is kicking my boy?' You feel as though people are thinking that such children should not be allowed to mix with 'ordinary' children. It is also totally baffling to understand this behaviour, since Alex is happy and contented. I assume it happens because he feels frustrated by his lack of communication skills, or perhaps he felt left out.

I have to say I have been overwhelmed with the support from our local mainstream school, where our son has attended since age 4.5. They have been marvellous, no negative attitudes, kind, helpful, reassuring and supportive. Our son has had the same non-teaching assistant since starting in the nursery there, which has been extremely beneficial for all of us. They have a special relationship. The school also tells me that our son is a clever little boy, and relatively speaking, he does well.

I am concerned that I may have been a bit negative in my comments. I must stress that we love our son and we do what we can for him. We would not change a hair on his head but we wish he wasn't handicapped.

Most days are normal busy days, as you have in any family, getting to school and work on time, and I don't suppose I feel any different from most other working mums.

I work three days a week, and I do not think I could manage a full-time job, running the home and taking Alex to his extra appointments like speech therapy and paediatrician checks. I want to be able to take him to these appointments rather than ask a carer to do it.

On the positive side, it can be rewarding bringing up a handicapped child as each achievement seems more of a reward because of the extra effort that most things require.

Our little boy is appealing, smiles a lot, and attracts a lot of attention when we are out. This can be very nice so long as he is behaving well.

I do feel sorry for my daughter, who is 19 months younger, because she is often in her brother's shadow. She is a very grown-up little girl because she has had to do things by herself and 'help' me. For instance, if our son ran off in the street, she had to stay by the car, or hold a shopping bag if I was having trouble.

I am philosophical about life now, and I realise there are far worse conditions that can affect your child and we are grateful that our son can walk, run—or perhaps not sometimes—swim, talk, read and laugh, just to mention some of his abilities.

In many ways he is very capable and we are extremely grateful that he is healthy and happy.

2. Alex at 17.5- November 2004

I thought it was about time I wrote some more on this subject. After all, Alex is now 17.5 years old.

I know this is 'the mother' talking, but life has changed so much in a positive way from those early years. Alex is a delight. Anxious to please, polite, helpful, tidy, conscientious and a real chatterbox. He loves going to school, adores his family and forms close bonds with his cousins and other relatives.

We have enjoyed Alex and Charlotte's company very much, and it has been and is a pleasure to take them shopping, on holiday and visiting friends—far different from those early years. Of course, we still wish Alex did not have that extra chromosome, but life is not too bad now.

When Alex was little, many people said that if one had to have a handicapped child, Down's syndrome is the best disability, because of their sunny disposition. I remember thinking, if someone else says that to me, I will scream, but I now know exactly what they mean and I think it is true. I have seen so many other types of disabilities and I think, poor parents, that must be so hard to deal with.

Of course, our worries now are for the future, when Alex leaves school in June 2006.

We must start seriously considering this. There are courses at local colleges like life skills, and of course residential colleges, but we do not feel Alex is ready for residential college yet.

If I ever hear of a new baby being born with Down's syndrome, I feel so sad, and I worry for the parents. This is because I will never forget how we felt in those early days. However, I would tell them it is nothing like as bad as you think it is going to be. Naturally, nobody wants this to happen, but people like Alex can teach you such a lot about life and people and how shallow and vain human beings can be.

A poem sent to us

A Heaven-Sent Child

A meeting was held quite far from Earth:
"It's time again for another birth."
Said the Angels to the Lord above,
"This special child will need much love.
His progress may seem very slow,
Accomplishment he may not show
And he'll require extra care from the folks he meets down there.
He may not run, or laugh, or play,
His thoughts may seem quite far away,
In many ways he won't adapt and he'll be known as handicapped.
So let's be careful where he's sent,
We want his life to be content.
Please, Lord, find the parents who will do a special job for you.
They will not realise right away this leading role they are asked to play,
But with this child sent from above,
Comes stronger faith and richer love,
And soon they'll know the privilege given
In caring from this gift from Heaven.
Their precious charge, so meek and mild,
Is Heaven's Very Special Child."

Many people have said to us, 'You must be very special to be sent a child like Alex.' Sceptics would scoff, but I did like to hear this.

One Final Word

To all new mothers of Down's syndrome babies, please, please, try not to despair. We can honestly say that having and raising Alex has been far and away a rewarding, loving experience and nothing like we had anticipated.

I read three quotes recently, two of which I have never heard before:

> The most precious gift we can offer anyone is our attention. When mindfulness embraces those we love, they will bloom like flowers.
>
> **Thich Nhat Hanh**

The second quote is from **Mother Teresa**:

> 'I know God will not give me anything I can't handle. I just wish that he didn't trust me so much.'

This quote is very poignant because a friend told me that God only lets you suffer what he knows you can cope with and I fully remember thinking, please don't give me anything else bad to cope with.

Finally, to sum up, I can use the following words to summarise raising Alex.

'What a wonderful life I've had! I only wish I'd realised it sooner.'

Colette

A few words from Alex, after I asked him about his life.

Hello Mum darling, I love my sister and Francis, I love my cat Daisy and Dad and you. I walk to Harborne on my own because I am working in British Heart Foundation shop.

I like this very much. I love going to the gym and I love going to the pub, I do karaoke at the pub. I play my guitar hero. I love my lie-in on the weekends.

I love to be Independent. I like working and walking to Harborne on my own.